パビリオン トウキョウ 2021

監修：和多利恵津子（ワタリウム美術館）
編集：TOTO出版

PAVILION TOKYO 2021

TOTO出版

パビリオンサイトマップ ｜ Pavilion site map

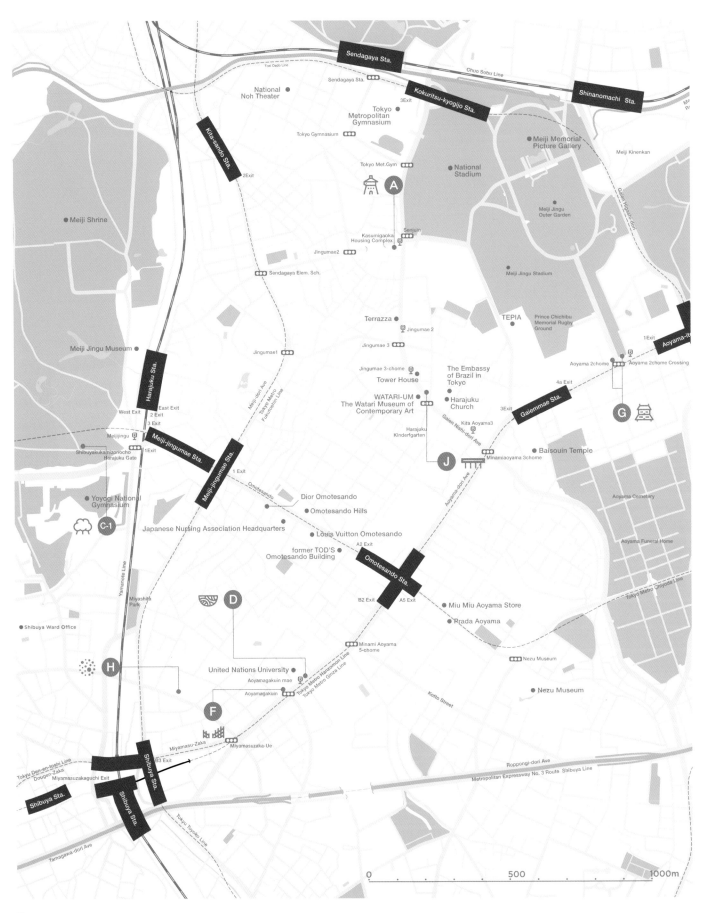

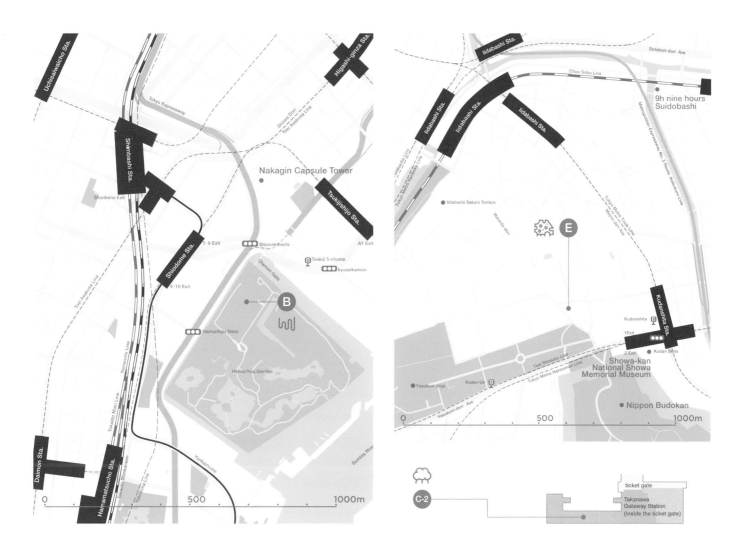

はじめに

2017年末、オリンピック・パラリンピックが開催される東京を、文化の面から盛り上げるために広くアイデアを求めた「Tokyo Tokyo FESTIVALスペシャル13」の一般公募が発表されました。「パビリオン・トウキョウ2021」（以降、本企画）は、2,436件の応募から採択されました。「パビリオン」という仮設の小さな建物や作品を都内各所に設置することで、「東京の新しいランドスケープをつくる」ことを目指していました。

本企画では、クリエイターのジャンルを取り払い、東京への想いを作品に込めてくれる方に参加を依頼しました。結果、活躍中の6人の建築家と3人の芸術家に決まり、設置場所、規模、素材はすべてクリエイター自身の希望に沿って決めていくことにしました。この方法は後に大変な困難をもたらすことになるのですが、それについては、あとがきで触れたいと思います。9つのパビリオンが徐々に現実のものとなる過程は、とてもワクワクする事件でした。

2020年に入り「コロナ禍」が広がると、多くの催しが中止と伝えられます。本企画は1年延期で開催が決定し、関係者間で「それならば、本気の場所をつくってみよう」という機運が高まりました。平素は頻繁に海外に出かけ不在がちなクリエイターたちも「コロナ禍」では東京に釘付けなので、とても丁寧な制作プロセスが実現しました。公開前夜に開催した開会式とバスツアー形式の記者発表には、主要なマスコミ関係者が集まりました。2021年7月1日、ついに一般公開がスタートし、見学者の様子を見ているうちに、これらのパビリオンはエンターテインメントでも、街を飾るパブリックアートでもない、何か別の役目をもって存在していることに気付き始めました。

本書は、2021年夏、東京に2か月だけ存在した9つのパビリオンの記録と共に、ここから次の東京へと進む何かの足がかりとなることを願い、刊行するものです。

本企画の実現には、多くの方の尽力がありました。巻末に、お力添えいただいた関係者のお名前を掲載し、心からの感謝を申し上げたいと思います。

和多利恵津子
パビリオン・トウキョウ2021 実行委員長 （ワタリウム美術館館長）

Preface

国際連合大学にて、開会式（2021年6月30日）。/ Opening ceremony at the United Nations University, June 30, 2021.

"Tokyo Tokyo Festival Special 13" was an initiative to promote Tokyo as a city of art and culture by offering a variety of cultural programs to spur cultural activities in the city where the Olympics and Paralympics were to take place. The open call for the project was announced at the end of 2017. The projects for "Pavilion Tokyo 2021," (hereinafter referred to as "this project") was selected from 2,436 entries. The aim of this project was to "create a new Tokyo landscape" by installing small temporary buildings and artworks called "pavilions" in various locations throughout the city.

For this project, we invited creators of all genres to participate, who were willing to convey their thoughts about Tokyo in their works. As a result, six architects and three artists active in their fields were chosen, and we decided that the location, scale, and materials of the installation were all decided according to the preferences of each creator. This approach would later lead to great difficulties, which I would like to discuss in the postscript. The gradual process of realizing the nine pavilions was a very exciting affair.

As COVID-19 pandemic spread into 2020, it was announced that a number of events were to be cancelled. This project was postponed for one year, and there was a growing momentum to "create truly special places" among those involved. Since the creators, who tended to go abroad frequently, were stuck in Tokyo due to the COVID-19 pandemic, they were able to carry out a careful production process. The opening ceremony and a bus-tour style press conference were held on the eve of the public opening, and were attended by major media outlets. On July 1, 2021, the pavilions finally opened to the public, and as I watched the visitors, I began to realize that these pavilions did not exist strictly for entertainment or as public art to decorate the city, but existed in some other capacity.

This book is a record of the nine pavilion that existed in Tokyo for only two months in the summer of 2021, and is published in the hope that it will serve as a stepping stone towards a better future for Tokyo.

The realization of this project was made possible by the efforts of many people. We would like to express our sincere gratitude to those who helped make this project possible by listing their names at the end of this book.

Etsuko Watari

Chairperson of Executive Committee of Pavilion Tokyo 2021,
Director of WATARI-UM, The Watari Museum of Contemporary Art

小さなパビリオンが大きな東京を救う

隈研吾
パビリオン・トウキョウ2021 名誉実行委員長（建築家）

大きいものは難しい。今回の東京オリンピック、パラリンピックの最大の教訓である。何しろオリンピックは大きい。世界で一番大きいイベントかもしれない。影響力の大きさもハンパない。会場もとてつもなく大きい。そういう大きなものに下手に関わると、大変なことになる。ひどい目にあう。国立競技場の設計コンペのやり直し、ロゴマークデザインの盗用騒ぎ、開会式プロデューサーの交代、等々「ひどい目」が果てしなく続いた。大きいものの困難さを、日本中の人間が目の当たりにし、思い知ったのである。

その難しさが何に由来するかを解き明かしていくと、1冊の現代社会論が書けるが、日本人の全員、あるいは地球上の多くの人が、大きいもののヤバさを、直観的に感じ取っただけでも、このオリンピックには、大きな歴史的な意味があったと僕は思う。まずインターネットによってすべてがつながったことが、この困難な状況を生んだ。地球の上のすべての情報がつながり、すべての人とものが、自由に地球上を移動する権利と手段を手に入れるという。この超流動的な状況の中で、大人数の集まるイベントを民主的な方法で、自由と平等を保証しながら管理運営することは、ほぼ不可能であることを、世界は学習した。理不尽なほどのコストをかけ、自由と平等を放棄するしかこの大きさをマネージできないのである。すなわち、この超流動性のもとでは、中国のような一種のサイバー独裁システムをもってしか、この種の大きなイベントのスムーズな運営は不可能なのである。

コロナがこの不可能性に拍車をかけた。逆の見方をすれば、コロナによって、この大きさを制限する言い訳ができたわけであり、コロナはコントロール不能の大イベントのマネージメントの一手段であったと見えないこともない。疫病というファクターの助けを借りなければならないほどに、大きいことの困難さは深刻で絶望的であった。

僕は国立競技場の設計に携わることで、この困難の渦の真ん中に投げ込まれ、大きいものの難しさを、いやというほどに味わうこととなった。ストレスは半端でなかった。しかし、僕がなんとかそれに耐えられたのは、大きいものに関わる一方で、小さいものにも携わり続けていたからである。小さなパビリオンを学生と一緒につくったり、小さな椅子や靴をデザインしたりという楽しい時間がなかったら、僕は、とっくのとうにつぶれていたと思う。

そして、僕がなんとかつぶれなかったように、東京という都市は、「パビリオン・トウキョウ2021」という小さなプロジェクトの併走によって、つぶれなかったように僕は感じる。東京の街角に、さまざまな小さなパビリオンをつくったり、小さなアートをつくるという試みを、ワタリウム美術館は1995年の「水の波紋展」以来、30年近く続けているのである。ワタリウムは、大都市が何を必要として

いるかを、知っているのである。

　「水の波紋」はバブルがはじけた後のしらけ切っていた東京で開かれた、ひとつの奇跡のような
アートイベントであった。ワタリウムがある東京の青山の街角のそこかしこに、アーティストが、小さな
アートを仕掛けた。バブル時代の、大きなプロジェクトがつくり出した、大味で殺風景な空間に辟易
していた僕らは、この「水の波紋」でほっとした。こんなやり方で都市に介入し、都市と付き合うや
り方があったんだということを知った。バブルで疲れ、乾ききっていた僕らにとって、「水の波紋」は、
文字通りにコップ1杯の水であり、この小さな水で東京は救われたのである。

　それは都市プロジェクトの意義を変えただけではなく、アートというものの定義をも変えたように
僕は感じた。従来アートとは、美術館という大きなハコの中に置かれ、閉じ込められていた。僕ら
も美術館というハコの中に入らなければ、アートと付き合うことが許されなかったのである。しかし
「水の波紋」は、アートを街に脱走させ、アートと僕らの両方に、自由と救いを与えてくれたので
ある。そこから始まった流れが、ついに「パビリオン・トウキョウ」という形をとって、大きなオリパラ
を救い、街で自由が生き残ったのである。

　その流れは青山という街とも関係している。20世紀という時代は、すなわち工業化の時代は、
大手町のような都心と、世田谷のような郊外の二項対立によって支えられていた。エリートは都心
の大きなビルで働き、静かな郊外の大きな家に住むのである。青山はどっちつかずの、いい加減な
場所で、神社とかお寺とか外苑の森のような、20世紀には収まりきらない異物、ノイズがちりばめ
られていた。そんな不思議な場所が気に入って、僕はこの30年間、ずっと青山を仕事場にしてい
るのである。その青山の街角が、「水の波紋」を自然に受け止め、「パビリオン・トウキョウ」の
サイトとなったのである。

　その意味で、「パビリオン・トウキョウ」とはひとつの事件である。大きなものが終わって、小さな
ものが始まるという事件。工業化という大きさが重要な時代が終わって、それにかわる小さな経済、
小さな文化が始まるという事件。大きな建築もアートも終わって、キラキラした小さな断片が、街に
散らばっていくという事件。大事件だけれど、小さな大事件。

Small Pavilions Save Big Tokyo

Kengo Kuma
Honorary Chairman of Executive Committee of Pavilion Tokyo 2021 / Architect

Big things are difficult. This is the biggest lesson learned from the Tokyo Olympics and Paralympics. After all, the Olympics is a big event. It may be the biggest event in the world. Its influence is tremendous. The venues are also enormous. If you get caught up in something that big, you will get into a lot of trouble. Terrible things might happen. In fact, there was an endless string of "terrible events" that occurred, including the redoing of the design competition for the National Stadium, the fiasco over the plagiarism of the logo design, and the replacement of the producer of the opening ceremony. People all over Japan witnessed and realized the difficulties of dealing with something so big.

I could write a whole book on modern society If I were to explain the origin of these difficulties. I do believe that this Olympics had a great historical significance, if only because all the Japanese people, or many people on this planet, intuitively sensed the seriousness of something so big. First of all, the fact that everything is connected by the internet has created this difficult situation. It has created a superfluous situation in which all the information on this planet is connected, and all people and things have the right and means to move around on this planet without restriction. The world has learned that in this superfluous situation, it is almost impossible to manage and organize a massive event with large crowds in a democratic way, while guaranteeing freedom and equality. It seems that the only way to manage an event of this magnitude is to impose unreasonable costs and abandon freedom and equality. In other words, under this superfluidity, only a cyber dictatorship of sorts, like that of China, can ensure the smooth operation of a major event like this.

The COVID-19 pandemic spurred this impossibility. Looking at it the other way around, however, the COVID-19 pandemic provided an excuse to limit the size of the event, and it is not hard to see that it was one of the effective ways to manage a major event on a massive scale beyond our control. The difficulty of being something so big was so serious and desperate that it had to be aided by the pandemic factor.

Having been involved in the National Stadium project, I was thrown into the middle of this chaos and experienced firsthand the difficulties of something so big. I was under tremendous stress. However, I managed to endure it because I kept working on small things as well as big ones. If it were not for the fun times I had building small pavilions with students and designing small chairs and shoes, I probably would have fallen apart long time ago.

Just as I have managed to stay afloat, I feel that the city of Tokyo has managed to stay afloat thanks to the small project "Pavilion Tokyo" that was underway at the same time. The Watari Museum of Contemporary Art has been engaged in creating various small pavilions and artworks on the streets of Tokyo for almost thirty years since the "Ripple Across the Water" exhibition in 1995. The museum understands what the big city really needs.

"Ripple Across the Water" was a miraculous art event held right after the bubble economy in the stagnant and empty atmosphere of Tokyo. Artists set up small artworks here and there on the streets in Aoyama, Tokyo, where the Watari Museum of Contemporary Art is located. Having been fed up with the dreary spaces created by large-scale projects during the bubble economy era, we felt a sense of relief by the "Ripple Across the Water" event. We realized that we could intervene and interact with the city in this way. For those of us exhausted by the bubble economy, the "Ripple Across the Water" was literally a glass of water, and this small amount of water saved the city of Tokyo.

It seemed to me that it not only changed the significance of urban projects, but also the definition of art itself. Traditionally, art has been confined within a big box called a museum, and we were only allowed to engage with art within the confines of a museum. However, "Ripple Across the Water" allowed art to escape into the city, bringing freedom and salvation to both the art and all of us. The trend that started there finally took the form of "Pavilion Tokyo," saving the big Olympic games, and allowing freedom to be kept alive in the city.

This trend is also related to the Aoyama area. The twentieth century, the era of industrialization, was supported by the dichotomy between the city center like Otemachi and the suburbs like Setagaya. The elites worked in the city center and lived in big houses in quiet suburbs. Aoyama was somewhat of a hodgepodge, a haphazard place scattered with strange and otherworldly things and noises that could not be contained in the twentieth century, including shrines, temples, and the forest of Jingu-gaien. I liked this strange place so much that I have been working in Aoyama for the past thirty years. The streets of Aoyama naturally accepted the "Ripple Across the Water" which now became the site for Pavilion Tokyo.

In this sense, Pavilion Tokyo is a singular event. It was a case of the end of big things and the beginning of something small. It was an event that marked the end of the era of industrialization, when size mattered, and the beginning of a new era of small economies and small cultures. It was an event that marked the end of big architecture and art, and saw a scattering of small sparkling fragments throughout the city. A big event, yet on a small scale.

目 次

Contents

茶室「五庵」

藤森照信

東京オリンピックに合わせて茶室をつくろう。茶室は世界にも類を見ないビルディングタイプとして多くの人に見てもらいたい。

400年前に定形化した伝統的茶室もいいが、フリースタイルの茶室の方が建築的面白さは大きい。

フリースタイルの茶室をこれまで日本と世界でいくつも手がけてきたが、せっかくだから何かひとつ新しいことをしよう。そう考えて思い至ったのは、地面が小さくポコッと隆起した上に載るテーブル式の茶室。

地上に穿たれた小さな入り口から潜り入り、暗い中を潜って茶室に上がると、視界が開け、オリンピックの巨大な競技場と東京の街の一画が見える。

夜になって明かりが灯ると、茶室というより大きな灯籠のような働きをするだろう。

茶室本体はJパネルでつくり、外側は焼杉を貼っている。炭という物質は土と並んで究極の建築材料にほかならない。なぜなら、すべての有機物は炭に帰るし、すべての無機物は風化の果てに土に至るからだ。

室内の壁にはJパネルが露出するが、天井にはJパネルの上に漆喰を塗り、その上に砕いた炭の小片を貼って仕上げる。外にも炭、中にも炭。

この茶室は立礼（テーブル式）だから、テーブルが大きな見せ場となる。信州の山から伐り出した栗の厚板を何枚も継ぎ、節や割れや歪みを積極的に生かして自然の木のもつ野性味を表立たせる。そしてテーブルに穴をあけて炉を入れ、水盤を埋めて花を活ける。

火と水は、400年前に利休が茶室というビルディングタイプをつくった時からの良きコンビ。

建築には珍しく茶室は人間のように自分の名をもつ。

"五庵"

Tea House "Go-an"

Terunobu Fujimori

Our idea was to build a teahouse in time for the Tokyo Olympics. Teahouse is a unique building typology unlike any other in the world, and we wanted many people to see it. While traditional teahouses that were established four hundred years ago are certainly impressive, we find free-style teahouses to be architecturally more interesting.

We have built a number of free-style teahouses in Japan and around the world, but given the opportunity, we felt we should try something new. So, we decided to build a table-style teahouse on top of a small rise in the ground.

After entering through a small entrance into the ground and passing through the darkness to the tearoom, the view opens up to reveal the enormous Olympic stadium and a glimpse of the Tokyo cityscape.

When lit up at night, it will function more as a large lantern than a teahouse.

The main body of the teahouse is made of J-panels (three-layered laminated wood panels with alternating grain patterns in perpendicular directions,) and the exterior is finished with burnt cedar. Charcoal, along with soil, is the ultimate building material. This is because all organic matter returns to charcoal and all inorganic matter returns to soil after weathering.

J-panels are exposed on the interior walls, while the ceiling is made of J-panels finished with plaster and small pieces of crushed charcoal on top of the plaster. As a result, there will be charcoal both on the outside and inside.

Since this tearoom is designed for a ryurei (table and chair style) tea ceremony, the table becomes the centerpiece. It is made by joining several thick chestnut boards cut down from the mountains of Shinshu. The knots, cracks, and distortions were intentionally used to highlight the raw beauty of natural wood. Holes were then drilled into the table to accommodate a furnace and embed a water basin in which flowers are arranged. Fire and water have always been a perfect combination since Rikyu created a building typology of the teahouse four hundred years ago.

Teahouses, unlike most buildings, have names of their own, just like people.

This teahouse is named Go-an.

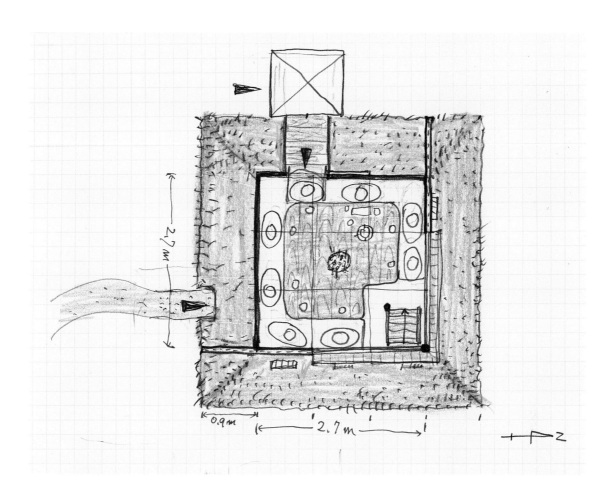

2.7 m

0.9 m ← 2.7 m →

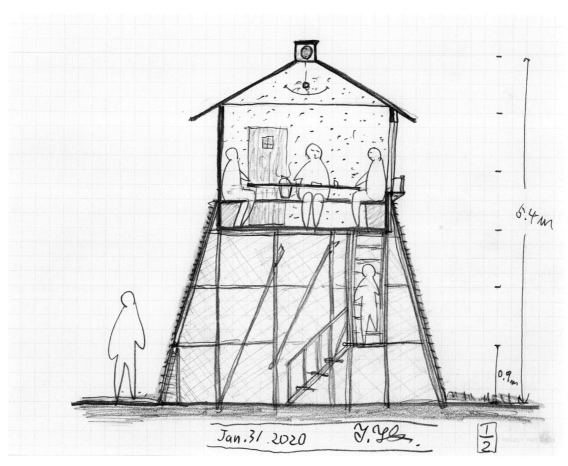

5.4 m

0.9 m

Jan.31.2020

1/2

GO-AN 2020

Jan.31 2020

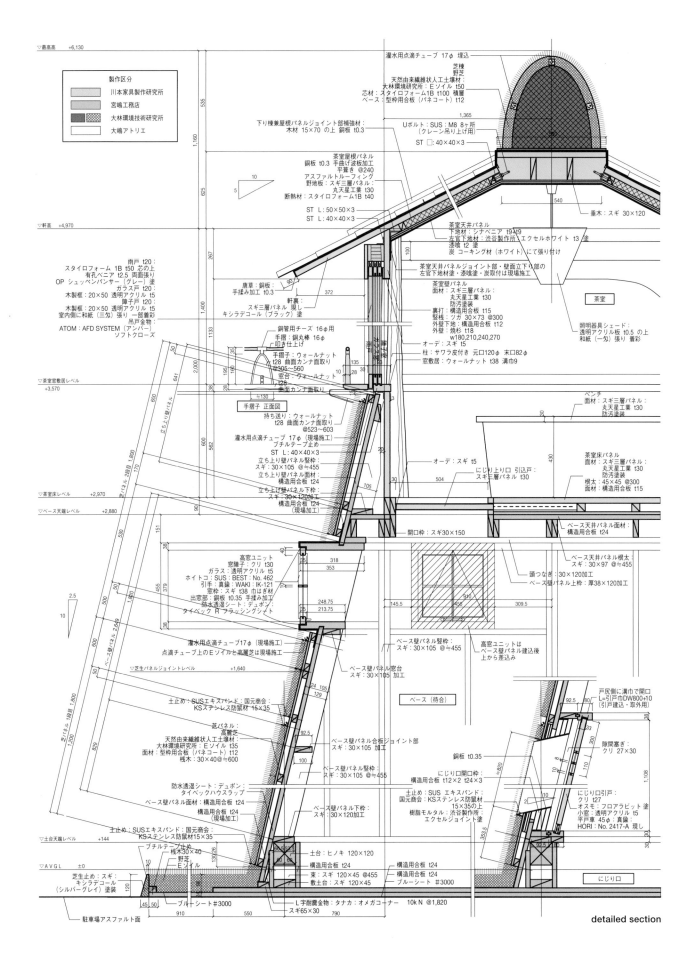

detailed section

18

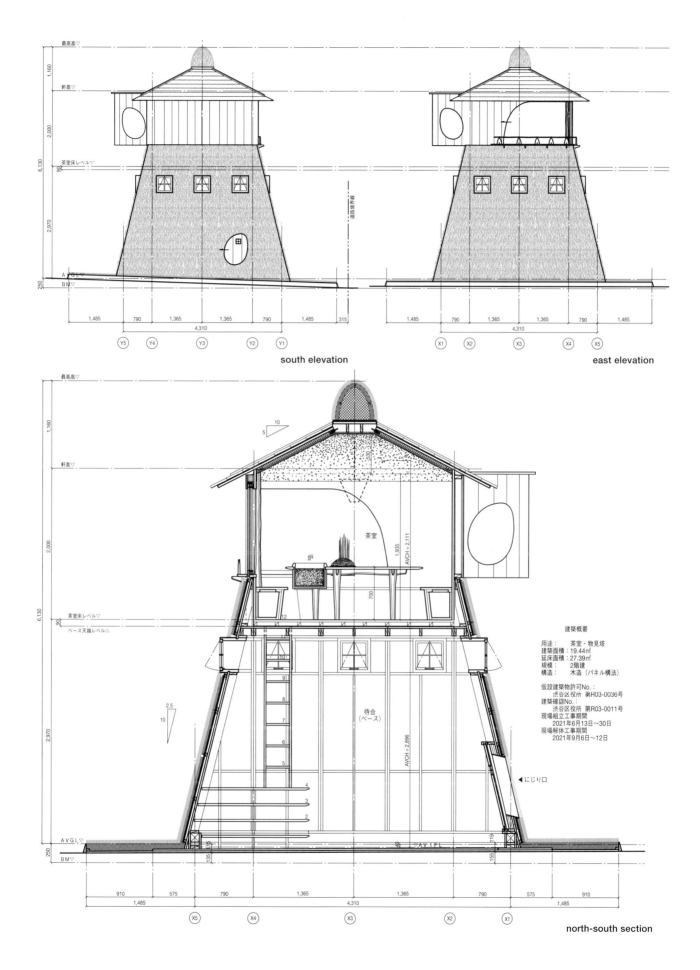

south elevation

east elevation

north-south section

建築概要

用途： 茶室・物見塔
建築面積：19.44㎡
延床面積：27.39㎡
規模： 2階建
構造： 木造（パネル構法）

仮設建築物許可No.：
　渋谷区役所 第H03-0036号
建築確認No.：
　渋谷区役所 第R03-0011号
現場組立工事期間
　2021年6月13日〜30日
現場解体工事期間
　2021年9月6日〜12日

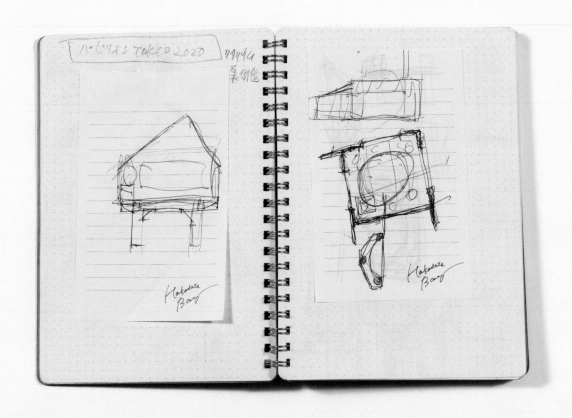

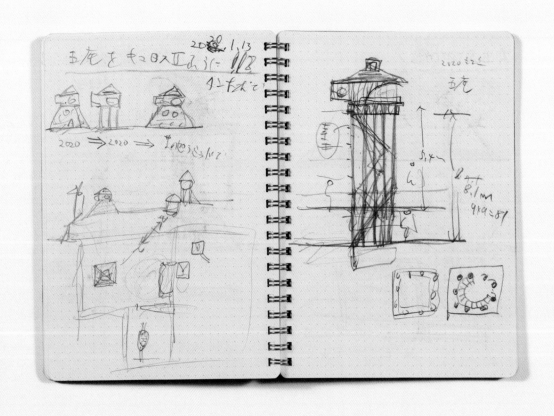

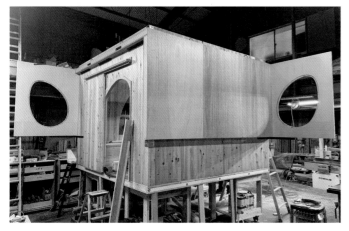

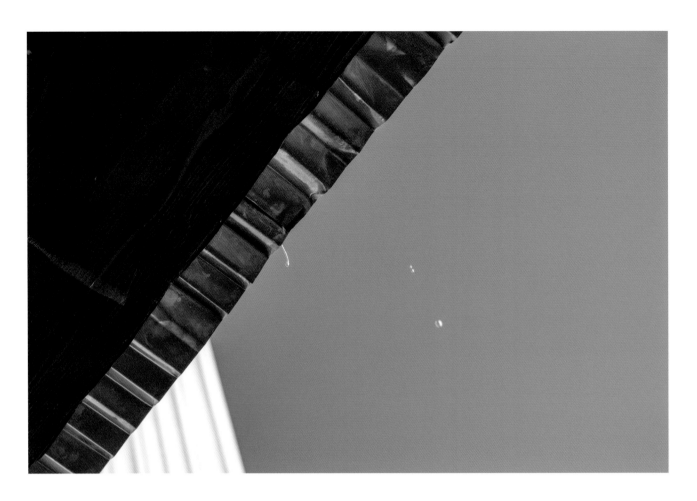

水明

妹島和世

まず歴史的な場所がいいだろうと考えました。過去を知り学び、次は未来に向けてつくっていく。そうやって過去と現在、そして未来はつながっているのだろうと思います。

浜離宮恩賜庭園は、江戸幕府の歴代将軍によって何度も造園、改修工事が行われた江戸時代を代表する大名庭園です。背後には新橋や汐留の高層ビル群がそびえ立っています。歴史と現代という東京のふたつの側面に触れられる場所だと確信しました。始まりは将軍家の鷹狩場で、昔は田舎だったのだと今でも何となく感じ、東京という都市の拡大を思います。その中でも、おもてなしの場所としてふさわしい、明治初期に整備された迎賓館「延遼館」の跡地を選びました。

浜離宮恩賜庭園は、海水を引き入れた潮入の池や、ふたつの鴨場など庭園を楽しむための多様な水場があり、水と共にある庭園だと言えます。その風景に現代を表すような水を足してみたいと考え、曲水（平安時代の寝殿造庭園にあった水路）をイメージして設計しました。

水はすべての生命にとってかけがえのないものであり、着物にも使われる流水文様は「苦難や災厄をさらりと流す」「流れる水は腐らず常に清らか」「お浄めや火難除」といった意味が込められます。

芝生の上に現れる水の流れは、遠くから見ると留まっているように見えますが、近づいて見ると静かに流れていることに気付きます。常に新しく変わりながら姿を留めている様子から、過去、現在、未来のつながりを表します。

鏡面の水路に浅く張られた水は、松や梅などの木々や周辺のビルを映してきらきらと輝きます。タイトルの「水明」は、澄んだ水が日や月の光で美しく輝く様子を示す言葉で、東京のこれまでを映しながらも常に変わり続ける水面から、清らかな未来を想像できるようにという期待を込めました。
鴨長明の『方丈記』の冒頭「行く川の流れは絶えずして、しかももとの水にあらず。淀みに浮ぶうたかたは、かつ消えかつ結びて、久しくとどまりたるためしなし。」という状況を表現できたらと思います。

Suimei

Kazuyo Sejima

First, we thought that a historical site would be ideal. Knowing and learning from the past, the next step is to create for the future. This is how the past, present, and future are connected.

Hamarikyu Gardens is one of the most prominent daimyo (feudal lord) gardens of the Edo period, having been landscaped and renovated many times by successive shoguns of the Edo Shogunate. The garden is set against the backdrop of soaring skyscrapers in Shinbashi and Shiodome. We were convinced that this was a place where one can experience two different aspects of Tokyo, the historical and the modern. It was originally a falconry site for the Shogun's family, and even now there is still a vaguely rural atmosphere that reminds us how the city of Tokyo has expanded over a long period of time. We chose the former site of Enryokan, a guesthouse built in the early Meiji period, which is a perfect place for welcoming people in the garden.

Hamarikyu Gardens is a garden closely associated with water, with Shioiri-no-ike, a tidal pond that draws in seawater, two duck hunting sites, and various other water features for enjoying the garden. We decided we wanted to add another water feature reflecting the modern era to the existing landscape, and came up with a design inspired by kyokusui, a waterway featured in the Heian period gardens.

Water is essential to all life. The ryusui (flowing water) pattern used on kimonos has the meaning of "water flushes away hardships and misfortunes," "flowing water never rots, and is always pure," and "water purifies and wards off fire."

From a distance, the flow of water across the lawn seems to be still, but upon closer look, one will notice that the water is flowing gently. The ever-changing yet ever-present appearance of the water represents the connection between the past, present, and future.

The shallow water in the mirrored waterway sparkles, reflecting the pine and plum trees, as well as the surrounding buildings. The title "Suimei" refers to the way clear water sparkles beautifully in the light of the sun or moon, and conveys our hope that the ever-changing water surface, while reflecting Tokyo's past and present, will help us imagine a bright and unsullied future.

"Hojo-ki" by Kamo no Chomei begins as follows: "Incessant is the change of water where the stream glides on calmly: the spray appears over a cataract, yet vanishes without a moment's delay." This is the situation that we wish to express.

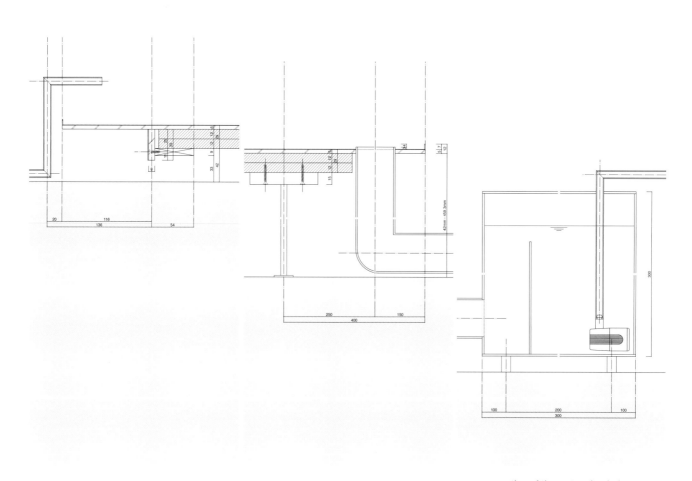

section of the water circulation system

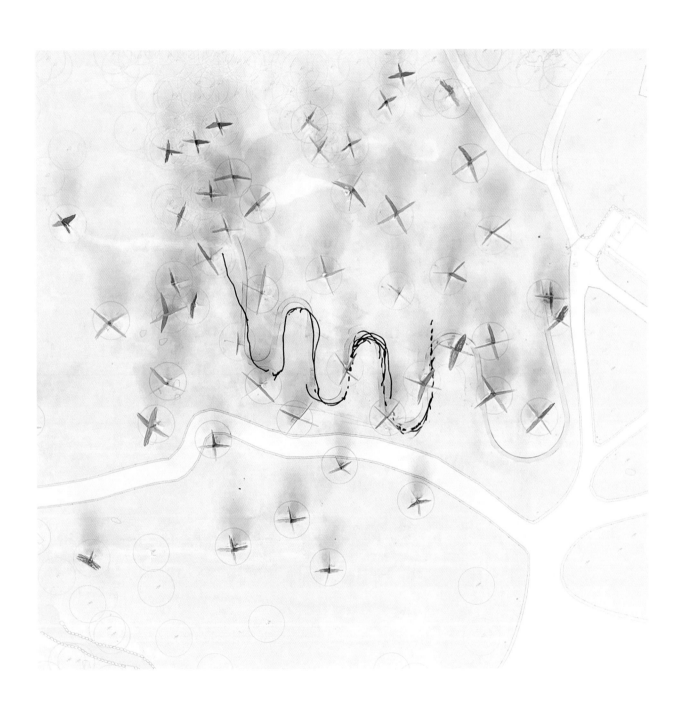

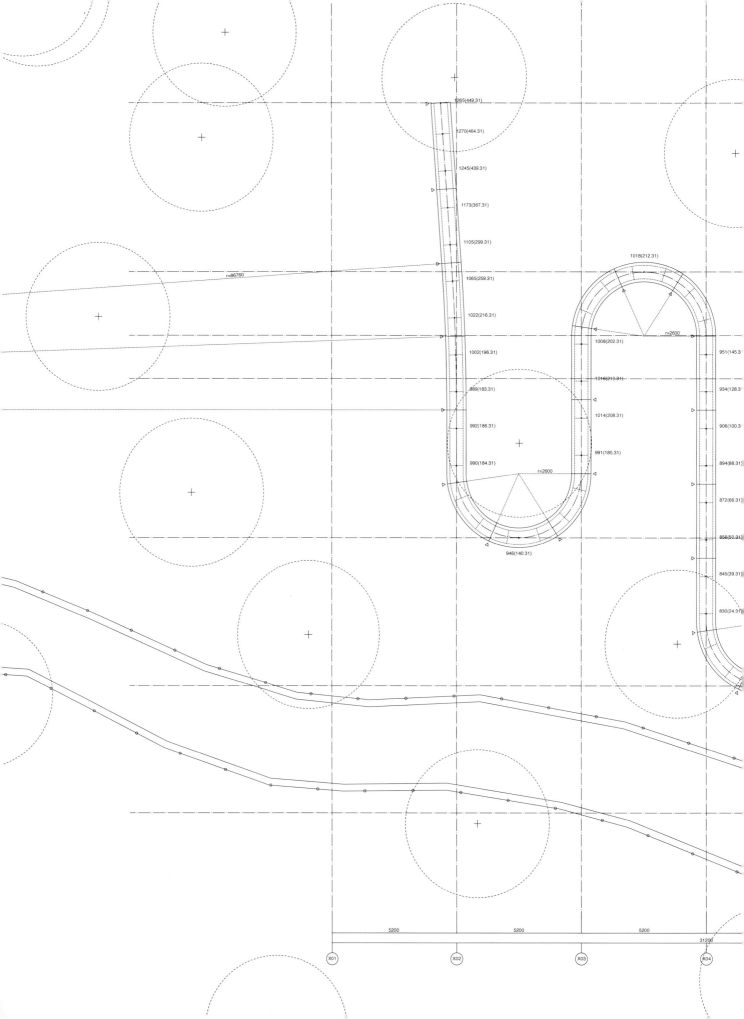

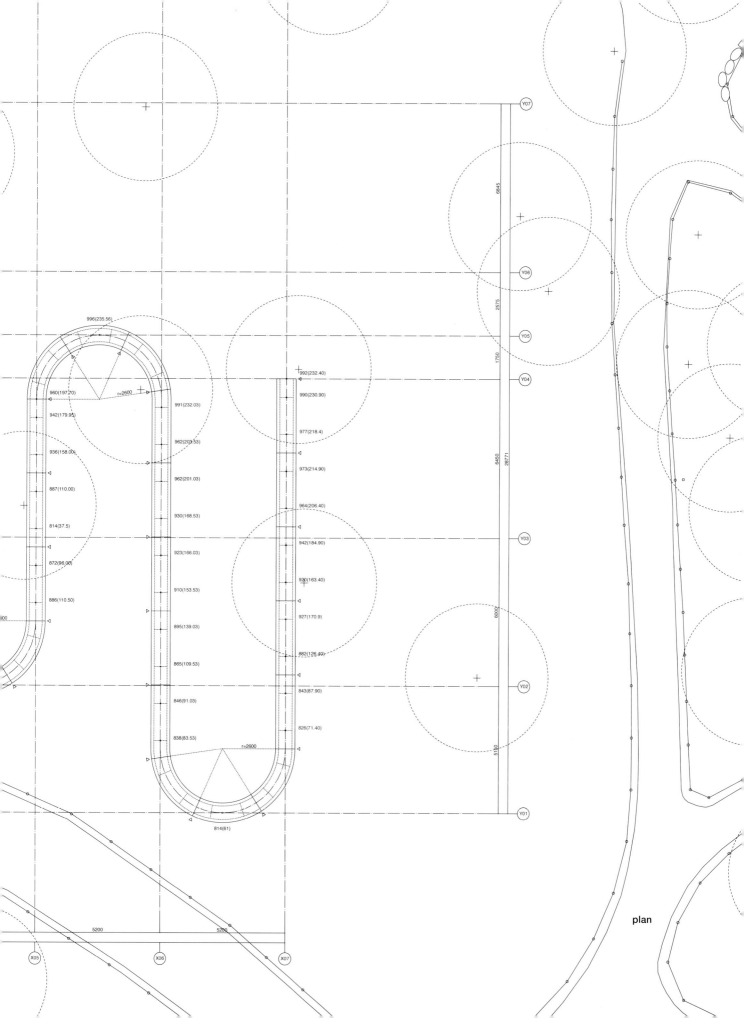

plan

Cloud pavilion（雲のパビリオン）

藤本壮介

究極の建築とは「雲」ではないでしょうか？

飛行機の窓から雲をよく見ると、雲には外観はありますが壁はなく、しかし内部空間は存在します。その内部空間は3次元的に非常にダイナミックで、建築では絶対に実現できませんが、建築的な何かがあるように感じさせる存在です。私たちを屋根のように覆ってくれる雲のようなものも、建築のひとつとして考えられるのではないでしょうか。それは、世界中のさまざまな国や地域や状況の上に浮かぶ「世界の大屋根」のような存在で、世界を統合と寛容によって包み込みます。

このパビリオンは、そのような「雲」にインスピレーションを受けて、「すべての人のための屋根 −Roof for All−」というコンセプトのもと、多様性と寛容性を象徴する場所として、東京オリンピック・パラリンピック期間中に、東京へと訪れる人びとのための出会いと休憩とコミュニケーションのための場所を提供します。

また、このパビリオンは緑豊かな場所と都市的な場所という複数の場所に設置されます。東京は非常に巨大な都市でありながら同時にヒューマンスケールで構築されています。大きなものと小さなものが相反するわけでなく、それぞれが互いを引き立て合ったり、混ざり合ったりして、両方がもっている価値観がうまく共存しています。個々の小さな成り立ちが、そのほかの小さな成り立ちと相互作用して、東京という都市の活気をつくり出しているように感じました。そのような意味合いの中で、パビリオンという小さな建築、小さな場所を都内各地に配置し、そこから何かを発信するということが、非常に東京的な発想だと受け止めました。そうして、同じものが異なる場所に置かれることによって、より一層それぞれの場所の違いや特性が引き立てられ、あぶり出されるのではないかと考えています。今回のプロジェクトは直接触る等のフィジカルに相互作用することは期待できませんが、一方でそれゆえ期待できる楽しみ方があると思います。気楽に通り過ぎてもいい、日陰として使ってもいい。そうして日常の中に位置付けられると良いなと思います。

Cloud pavilion

Sou Fujimoto

Perhaps we could say that the ultimate architecture is "clouds."

If you look at a cloud closely from an airplane window, you will see that it has an exterior form, but no walls, yet there is a space inside. Its interior space is very dynamic and expansive in three dimensions, and seems to possess some architectural quality, although it is something absolutely impossible to achieve in architecture. Perhaps a cloud-like substance covering us like a roof can be considered a form of architecture. It floats above various countries, regions, and situations around the world like a "great roof of the world," and envelopes the world with unifying and receptive qualities.

Drawing inspiration from such "clouds," this pavilion is designed as a symbol of diversity and tolerance under the concept of "Roof for All," providing a place for people visiting Tokyo during the Tokyo Olympics and Paralympics to meet, rest, and communicate.

This pavilion is placed in several locations, in both green and urban areas.
Tokyo is a vast metropolis, yet at the same time it is built on a human scale. The big and the small do not conflict with each other, but they complement and mix with each other, allowing their respective values to coexist in harmony. It seems to us that each small component interacts with other small components to create the vitality of the city of Tokyo. In this sense, the idea of placing pavilions, or small buildings and small places, in various parts of the city, and disseminating messages from there, seems to be in line with the character of Tokyo. By placing the same object in different places, we believe that the differences and characteristics of each place will be further enhanced and revealed.

While this project does not allow physical interaction, including direct touch, there are many other ways to enjoy it. You can pass through it casually, or use it as a shade. We hope it will become a part of your daily life.

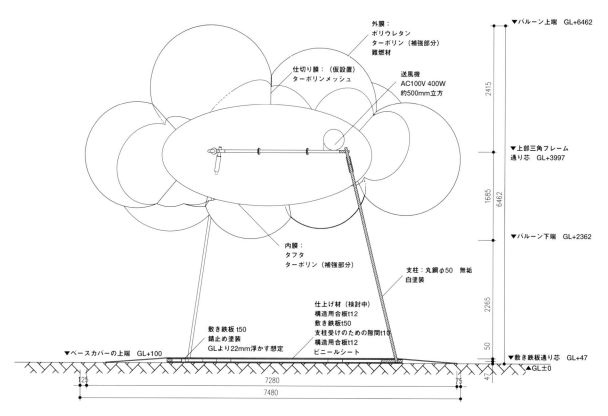

外膜：
ポリウレタン
ターポリン（補強部分）
難燃材

仕切り膜：（仮設置）
ターポリンメッシュ

送風機
AC100V 400W
約500mm立方

▼バルーン上端　GL+6462

2415

▼上部三角フレーム
通り芯　GL+3997

1685

6462

▼バルーン下端　GL+2362

2265

内膜：
タフタ
ターポリン（補強部分）

支柱：丸鋼φ50　無垢
白塗装

仕上げ材（検討中）
構造用合板t12
敷き鉄板t50
支柱受けのための隙間t10
構造用合板t12
ビニールシート

敷き鉄板 t50
錆止め塗装
GLより22mm浮かす想定

▼ベースカバーの上端　GL+100

50

▼敷き鉄板通り芯　GL+47

47

▲GL±0

125

7280

75

7480

section

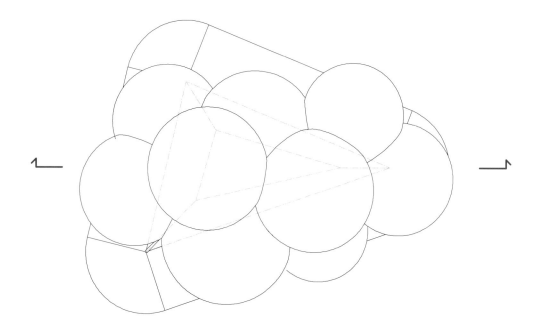

plan

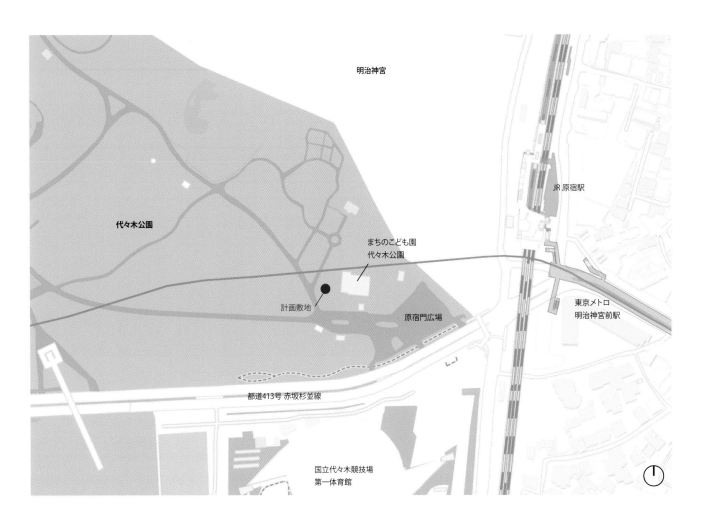

明治神宮

JR 原宿駅

まちのこども園
代々木公園

代々木公園

計画敷地

原宿門広場

東京メトロ
明治神宮前駅

都道413号 赤坂杉並線

国立代々木競技場
第一体育館

Yoyogi park

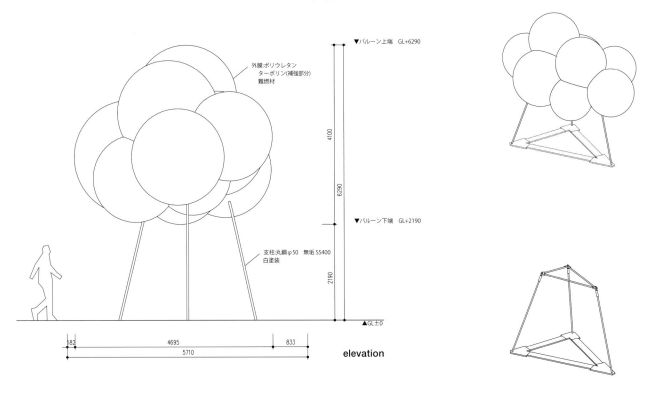

外膜:ポリウレタン
ターポリン(補強部分)
難燃材

▼バルーン上端　GL+6290

4100

6290

▼バルーン下端　GL+2190

支柱:丸鋼 φ50　無垢 SS400
白塗装

2190

▲GL±0

182　4695　833
5710

elevation

Takanawa Gateway station

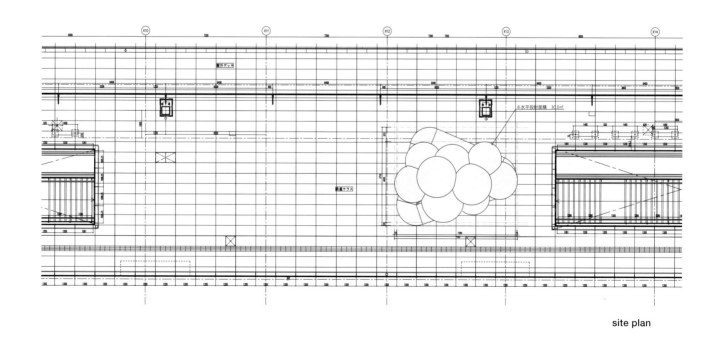

site plan

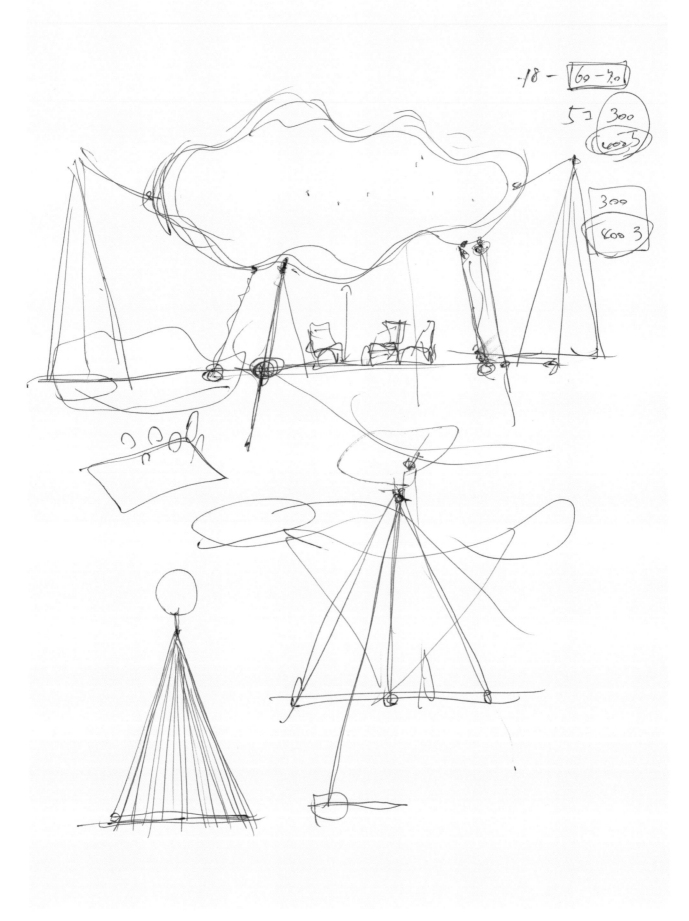

Edouard Glissant

全世界論

肉体性の科学

cloud roof.

ten

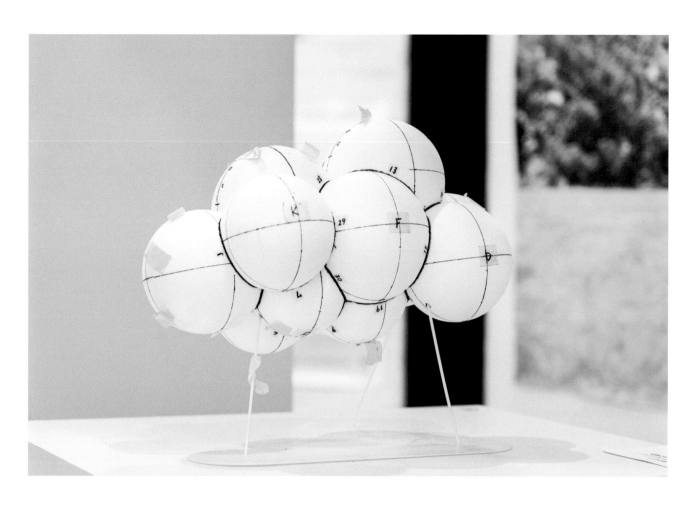

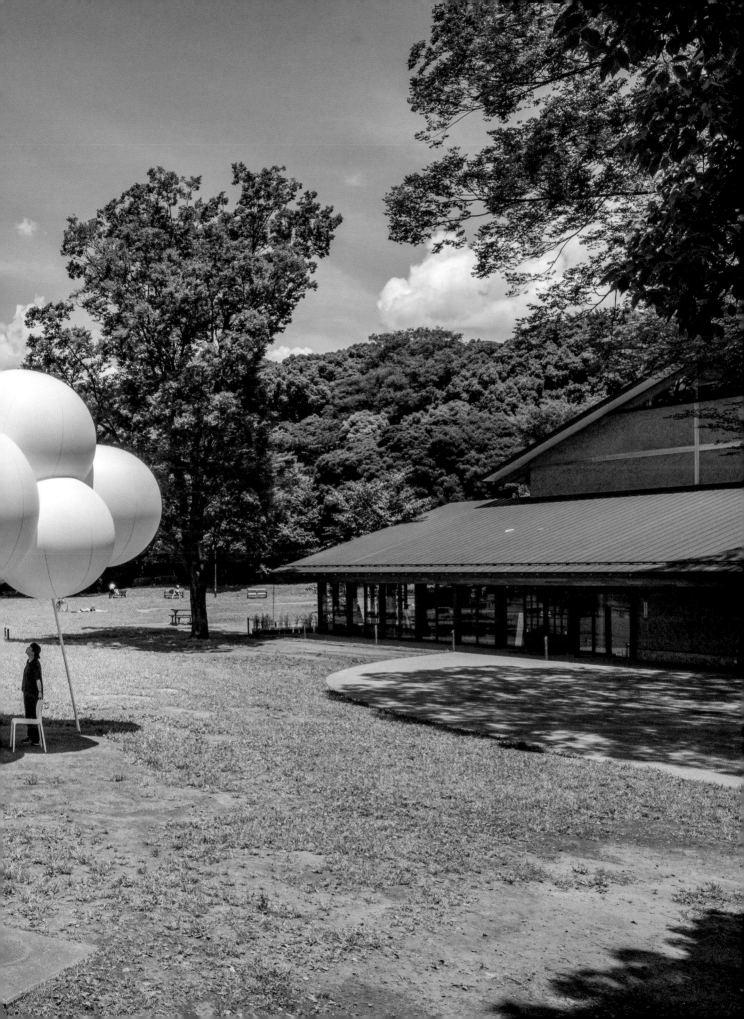

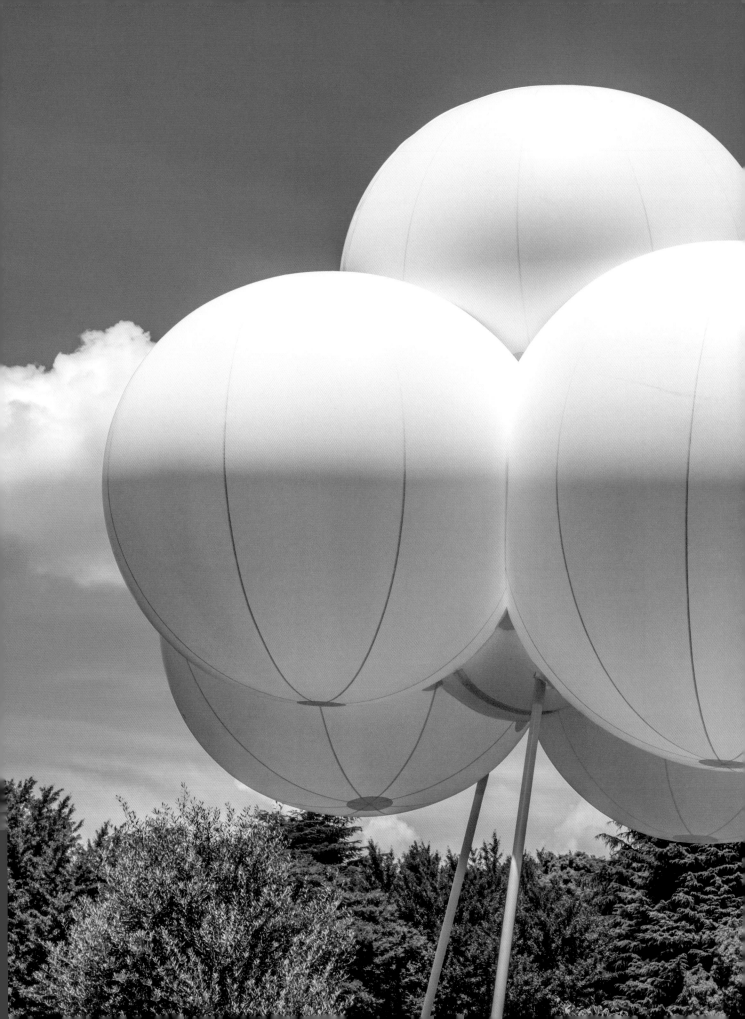

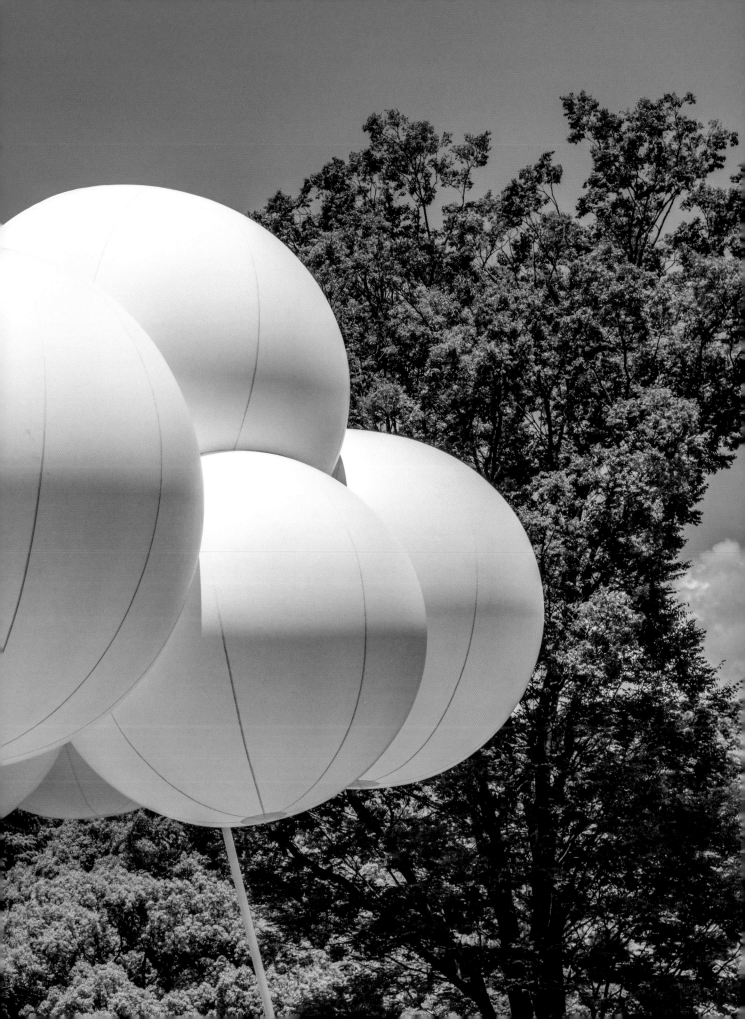

Global Bowl

平田晃久

たとえば樹上を自由に行きかう動物たちのように、人間が動物的本性を解放して行動できるような建築をつくること。それが僕の建築のテーマです。〈からまりしろ〉（「からまる」余地＝「しろ」）というのがその時のキーワードです。人びとの動物としての感覚を呼び覚ます、3次元的な〈からまりしろ〉は、どこかツルツルピカピカした状態になっていきがちな現代都市の中に、手触りのある異質性、あるいは「ひだ」をつくり出すでしょう。

未来の都市は、動物としての人間に開かれたものであってほしい、そう思っています。世界の人びとに開かれて企画された「パビリオン・トウキョウ」では、国籍や文化、人種や性別の差を超えて、種としての人間が動物としての喜びを共有できる場所をつくりたいと思いました。オリンピックスタジアムと比べてはるかに小さくとも、ボウル（お椀）のような形をつくることで、かえって坩堝（るつぼ）のような強度をもった「動物たち」の〈からまりしろ〉ができるのではないかと。

人びとが互いの身体を介して、喜びを分かち合う機会が失われている2021年のこの状況は、皮肉というほかありません。しかし、だからこそ、そんなシーンを「待ち続ける」このパビリオンは、意味をもったモニュメントとなるのかもしれません。生身の身体を介して人びとが集まる場の楽しさや重要性を決して忘れない、という決意の表れとして。また、コロナに打ち克つだけでなく、地球規模で起こっている根本的な矛盾に向き合う意志の表れとして。

孔だらけのボウルは、内外の境界をほどきつつ結ぶ、反転する幾何学でできています。つまり、都市の中に小さな閉域をつくりながら、同時に外側とつながるのです。国際連合大学前の敷地は、隣接する公開空地と湾曲する青山通りがつくり出す、都市の巨大なボイドが感じられる場所です。このパビリオンは観測装置のように、このボイドのへそのような位置に置かれます。

木材を3次元カットして組み合わせる、日本の最新技術を生かした建築が、力強い物質感と工芸品のような緊張感をもって立ち上がり、都市の中にさまざまな文脈を引き寄せる、孔のような場所が生まれるでしょう。

Global Bowl

Akihisa Hirata

To create architecture that allows humans to unleash their animal instincts and act as if they are animals freely roaming in the trees. This is the theme of our architecture. "Karamarishiro", or a "margin or room for something to tangle onto ("karamaru" means "to tangle," and "shiro" means "margin" or "room") is the keyword, and the three-dimensional "karamarishiro" that awakens our senses as animals will create a tactile heterogeneity or "folds" in modern cities that tend to become somewhat smooth and shiny.

We hope that cities in the future will be more open to humans as animals. With "Pavilion Tokyo," which was designed to be open to people from all over the world, we wanted to create a place where humans as a species could share the joy of being animals, transcending differences in nationality, culture, race, and gender. Even though it is much smaller than the Olympic stadium, by creating a bowl-like shape, we can create a "karamarishiro" for animals, with the strength of a crucible.

It is only ironic that the year 2021 has seen the loss of opportunities for people to share their joys through physical interaction with each other. However, perhaps this is why this pavilion, which continues to await such moments, will become a significant monument. It is an expression of our determination to never forget the joy and significance of places where people can get together in person. Moreover, it is also an expression of our will to not only overcome the Covid-19 situation, but also to confront the fundamental contradictions that are occurring on a global scale.

The perforated bowl is made of an inverted geometry that unravels and connects the boundaries between inside and outside. This means that it creates a small closed area within the city while connecting it to the outside at the same time. The site in front of the United Nations University is a place where one can feel the enormous void in the city created by the adjacent public open space and the curving Aoyama-dori Avenue. This pavilion is placed at the navel of the void, like an observation device.

The architecture, utilizing Japan's latest technology to cut and combine wood in three-dimensions, stands with a strong sense of materiality and a craft-like tension, creating a porous place that draws in various contexts into the city.

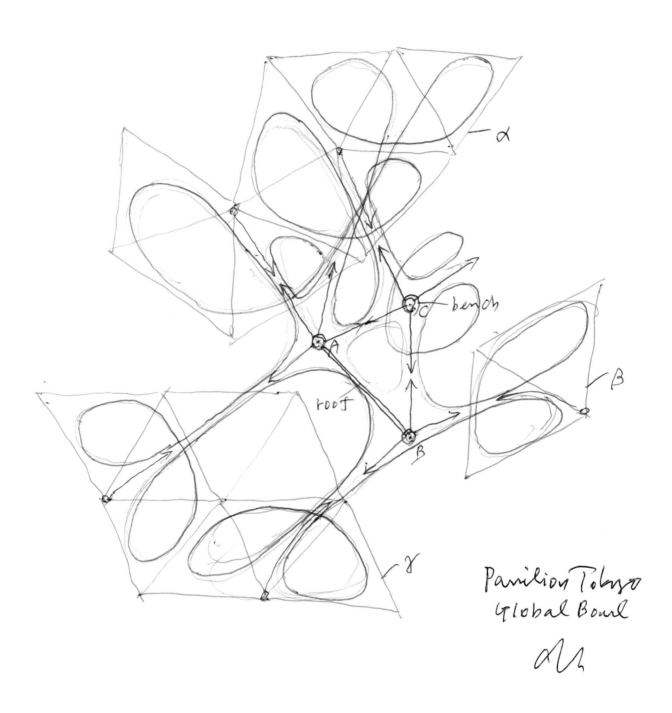

α

bench

C

A

roof

β

B

γ

Pavilion Tokyo
Global Bowl

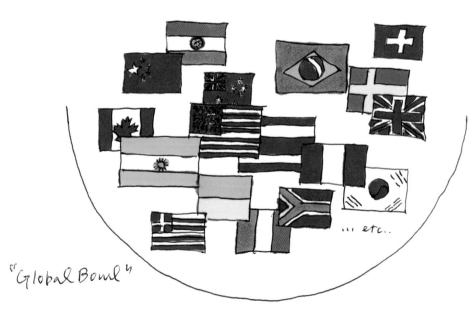

"Global Bowl"

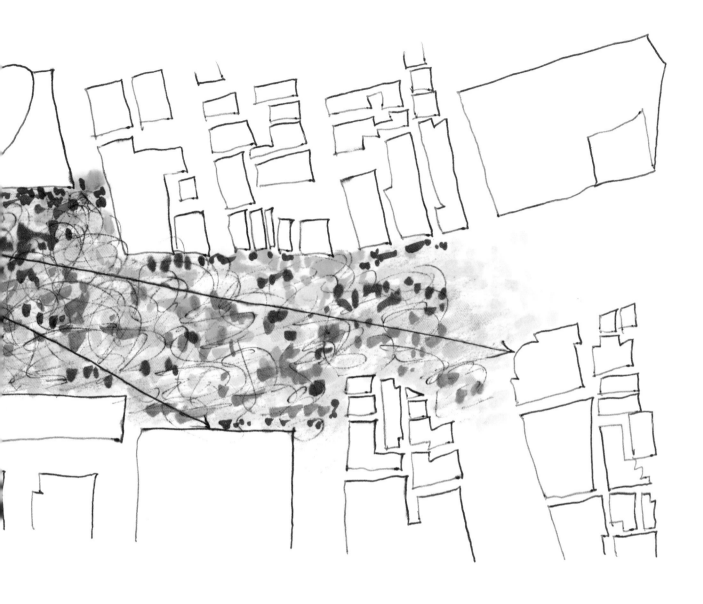

Pavilion Tokyo
Global Bowl

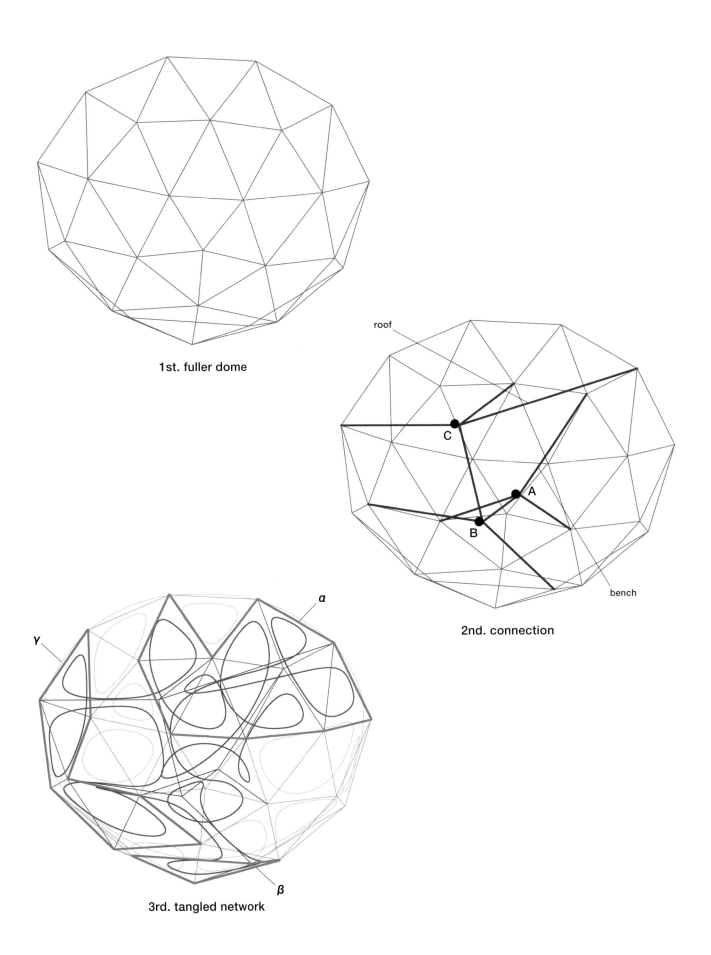

1st. fuller dome

roof

C

A

B

bench

2nd. connection

γ

α

β

3rd. tangled network

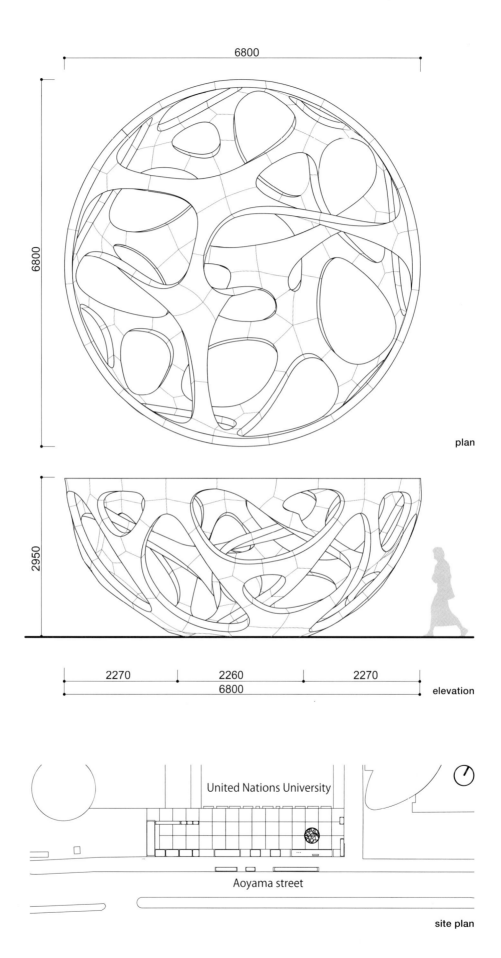

6800

6800

plan

2950

2270   2260   2270
6800

elevation

United Nations University

Aoyama street

site plan

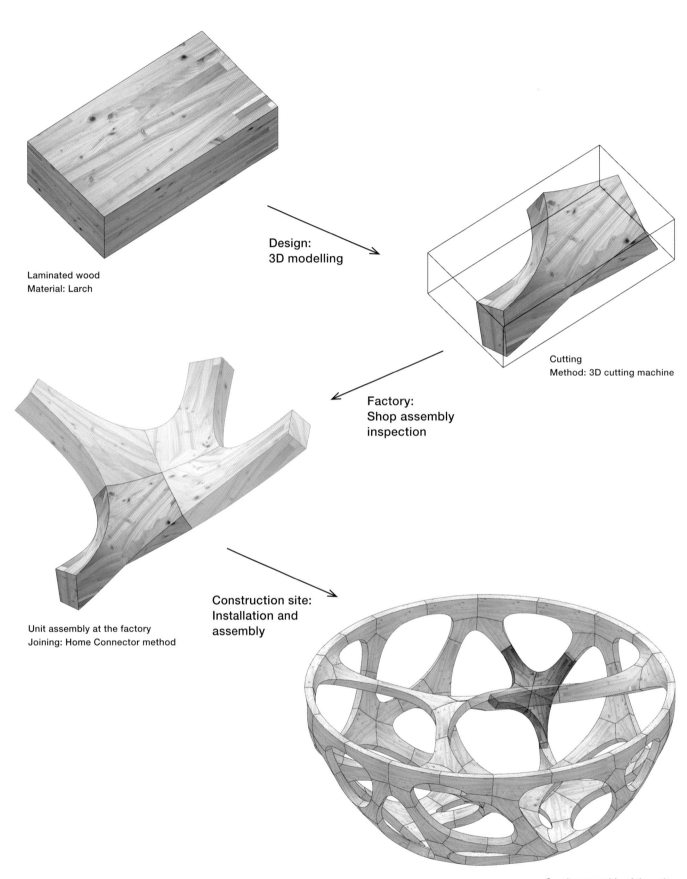

Laminated wood
Material: Larch

Design:
3D modelling

Cutting
Method: 3D cutting machine

Factory:
Shop assembly
inspection

Unit assembly at the factory
Joining: Home Connector method

Construction site:
Installation and
assembly

On-site assembly of the units
Joining: Screw joining

木陰雲

石上純也

九段に昭和2年、実業家の山口萬吉によって建てられた古い邸宅がある。設計には東京タワーの構造計画を行った内藤多仲も関わっている。この邸宅にある古い庭。今は高層建築に囲まれ、萎縮し、薄暗くなってしまっている。この庭の本来の美しさを取り戻すための建築を考える。

新しく計画される建築が、歴史ある風景に溶け込むように、新築であるにも関わらず、初めから古さを含みもつようにと考えた。具体的には、木造の柱と屋根を庭いっぱいに計画し、その構造体を焼き杉の技術を用いて焼いていく。さまざまに火力を調整しながら、杉の表面を炭化させ、場所によっては構造体そのものを焼き切る。庭に広がる木の構造体が、既存の庭に生い茂る老木を避けるように、焼かれながらしなやかに形状が整えられていく。炎で炭化した真っ黒の構造体は、廃墟のような趣もある。新築から廃墟の状態に、瞬時に駆け抜け変化したようでもあり、建築が経年によって得られる移り変わりを一気に獲得したかのようだ。

昭和初期にはまだ存在していなかった周りの高層建築を黒い構造体が覆い隠し、ビルに囲まれて薄暗くなってしまった庭の照度をあえて落とし翳りを導き、構造体に開けられた無数の穴から射し込む無数の光の線を美しく強調する。それはまるで日本家屋の暗がりから坪庭の弱く美しい光を眺めるようである。庭を取り囲む現代の風景は消え去り、弱々しい光が生き生きと輝き、訪れる人びとは美しさを取り戻したこの庭に流れる古い時間の中へ静かに溶け込んでいく。

真っ黒の構造体は、美しく際立つ弱い光の中で老木の間をゆったりと漂う暗がりとしての影である。

Kokage-gumo

Junya Ishigami

There is an old mansion in Kudanshita built in 1927 by industrialist Mankichi Yamaguchi. Tachu Naito, who undertook the structural engineering of Tokyo Tower, was also involved in the design. In this beautiful old garden of the mansion, a sunshade canopy gently shielding the sun was designed which was intended to be erected for a limited time in the summer of 2021.

In order to blend the newly built canopy into the historic landscape, we decided to infuse it with a hint of the old from the beginning even though it was a new structure. Specifically, wooden pillars and roofs were placed to fill the garden, and the structure was burnt using the traditional yakisugi (charred cedar) technique. By carefully adjusting the heat intensity, the surface of the cedar was charred, and some parts of the structure were burned off. The wooden structure spreading out in the garden was flexibly shaped as it was burned to avoid the old trees growing densely in the existing garden. The jet-black structure charred by flame has the appearance of a ruin. It seems to have changed from a new building to a ruin in an instant as if it had underwent changes that architecture goes through over a period of time.

The jet-black structure obscures the view of the surrounding buildings that did not exist in the early Showa period, and numerous particles of light penetrating through the countless holes in the structure blend with the sunlight filtering through the trees. The modern cityscape glimpsed through the trees disappears, the intense summer sunlight eases off, and visitors immerse themselves in the old time flowing in this garden. The jet-black structure is a cool shadow drifting among the old trees on a summer afternoon.

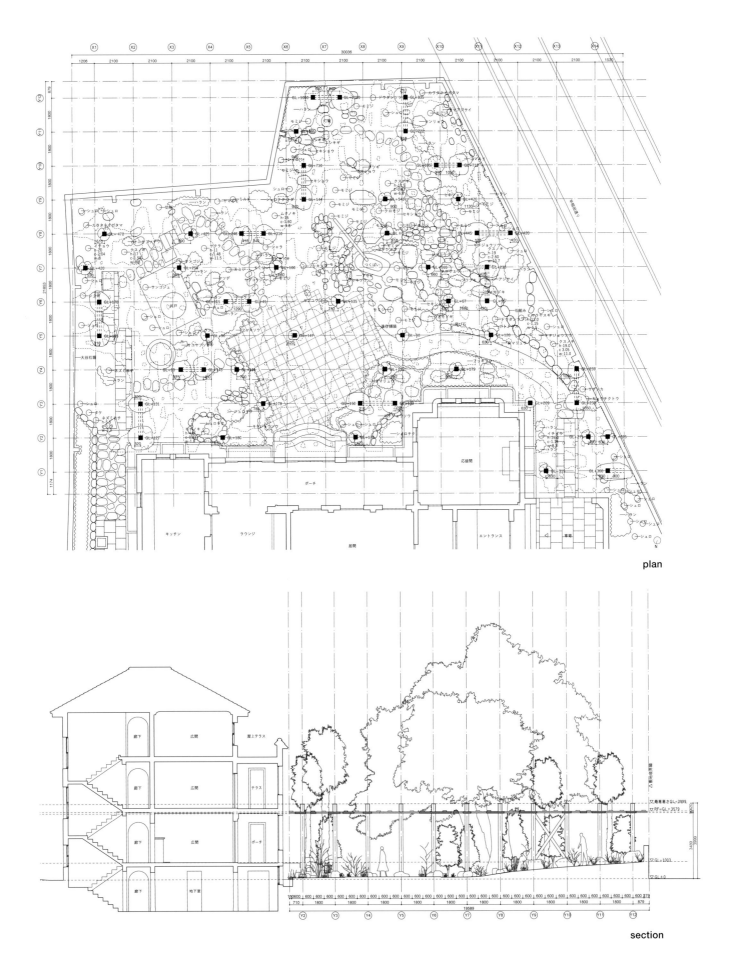

plan

section

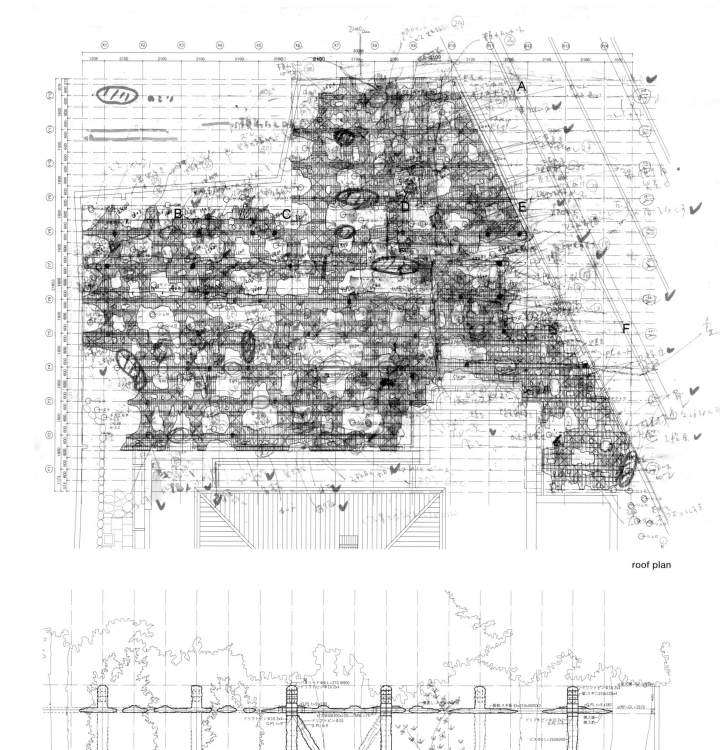

roof plan

detailed section

ストリート ガーデン シアター

藤原徹平

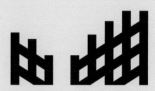

この1年間で考えたこと

ちょうど1年ほど前、コロナ禍は収まらず、オリンピックの1年延期が決定。パビリオン・トウキョウも2021年に延期されることになった。

単に1年ずれただけでなく、私には世界のバランスがもっと全体的に崩れているようにも感じられた。(例えば、もしもオリンピック自体が中止になったとしても、それが大きい出来事とは多くの人は感じないだろう。)

こうした世界の変化を受けて、私はパビリオンのコンセプトを変えることにした。

ストリートに着目するという着想そのものは変わっていないが、そこに植物の視点、人間以外の存在を加えて考えた。

人間が苦しんできたこの1年、植物はまるで影響を受けていないように見える。人間の活動が弱まったせいか、ずっと家にいるせいか、私は植物に目を向ける機会が以前よりずっと増えてきている。東京という都市の歴史を植物にこだわって調べていくと、庭が重要な存在であるということがクリアになってきた。江戸時代、大名たちが何百もの屋敷を構え、その屋敷には必ず庭園がつくられた。そのごく一部が、新宿御苑、有栖川公園などの重要な都市公園として残るが、そうした庭園が何千もひしめき合っていたのだから、江戸はまさに「庭の都」「植物の都」だった。

将軍や大名たちだけが、植物を愛でていたかというと、そうではないのが面白いところで、長屋住まいの庶民たちも自分たちだけの庭を育んでいた。

それを可能にしたのが、大名たちの庭を手入れする大量の植木職人たちの出現と、格安の植木鉢の登場、そして江戸の行商文化である。

今も東京では路地裏に入り込むと植木鉢が道や建物を埋め尽くすような風景に出くわすことがある。これは東京という都市が、階級差を越えて庭園を愛でる都市になっていったその歴史の痕跡である。植木は、東京という都市の最小スケールの秩序と言ってもよいかもしれない。このパビリオンを通じて、東京の植物と道にまつわる物語を提示しようと思う。

東京という都市に脈々と流れる、植物と人間がつくってきた循環的な関係。ローム層の肥沃な土が可能にした、都市の路地裏で農を営む都市。

このストリートパビリオンは、自分たちの日常をたくましく耕し続けてきた東京の市民文化に捧げられた、ひと夏の都市計画として提示される。この都市の文化の根っこが肥大化し、瘤のように隆起した異質空間、位相がずれてしまった世界のバランスを元に戻すのではなく、別の秩序に移行するきっかけになれば面白いと考えている。

2021年2月23日 2度目の緊急事態宣言下の東京

STREET GARDEN THEATER

Teppei Fujiwara

Thoughts over the Past Year

Just about a year ago, a decision was made to postpone the Tokyo Olympics for a year due to the ongoing COVID-19 pandemic. Accordingly, the Pavilion Tokyo was also postponed to 2021. Besides the one-year delay of the project, it seemed to us that the entire world was losing its balance. (For example, even if the Olympics was to be cancelled altogether, most people would not consider it a big deal.)
Given these changes in the world, we decided to change the concept of the pavilion.
While the idea of focusing on the street stayed the same, the perspective of plants and non-human beings were incorporated into our design process.
During the past year of human suffering, plants seem to have been entirely unaffected. Perhaps because of the decline in human activity, or perhaps because we spend most of our time at home, we tend to pay much more attention to plants than before.
As we researched the history of the city of Tokyo with a particular focus on plants, we realized that the gardens were an essential part of the city. During the Edo period, feudal lords built hundreds of mansions, each of which had its own garden. While only a fraction of these gardens remain as important urban parks today, including Shinjuku Gyoen and Arisugawa Park, Edo was once the "city of gardens" and "the city of plants," with thousands of such gardens clustered together.
It is interesting to note that shoguns and feudal lords were not the only ones who cherished plants; the common people living in row houses also cultivated their own gardens.
This was made possible by the advent of a large number of gardeners who tended the gardens of the daimyo (feudal load), the introduction of inexpensive flowerpots, and the peddling culture of Edo.
Even today, when one wanders into the back alleys of Tokyo, one may come across flowerpots lining the streets and buildings.
These are historical traces of how Tokyo became a city of garden lovers, transcending the divide between classes. One could say that gardening is an order of the smallest scale in the city of Tokyo, and through this pavilion, we would like to convey a story about plants and the streets of Tokyo.
In this city, plants and people have created a cyclical relationship that flows continuously, and the fertile soil of the loam layer has helped create a city where people grow crops in back alleys.
This street pavilion was proposed as a summer urban project dedicated to the civic culture of the city of Tokyo which has cultivated its own daily lives with great resilience. The roots of the city's culture grow and rise up like a rhizome, creating a heterogeneous space. We think it would be interesting if this pavilion could trigger a shift to a new order, rather than restoring the balance of the world that has gone out of phase.

Tokyo under the second COVID state of emergency, February 23, 2021.

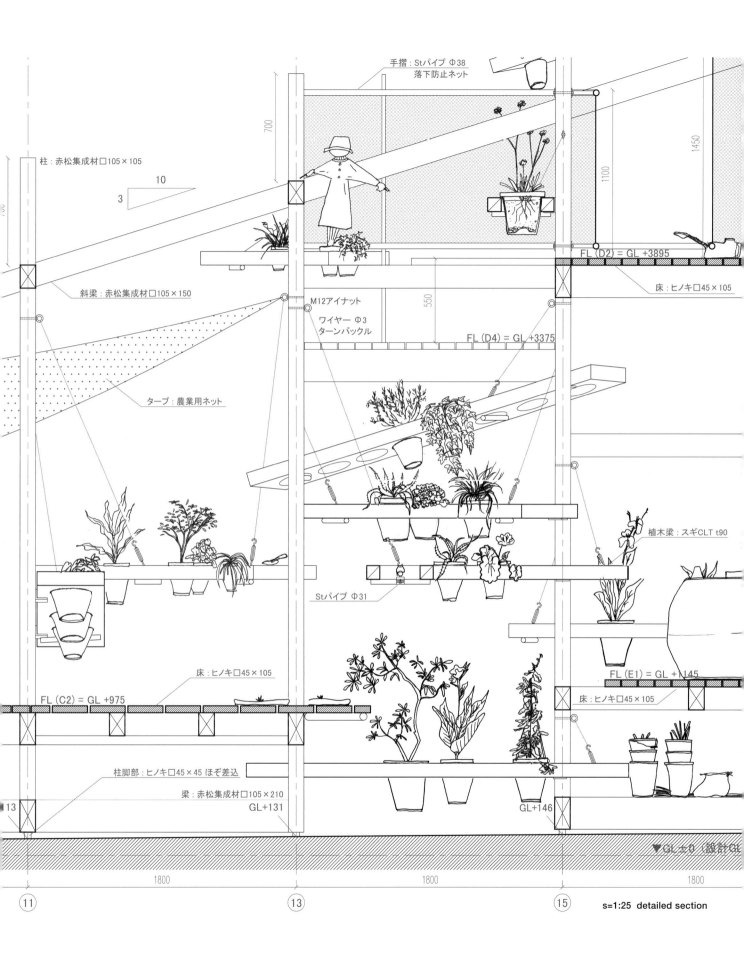

柱：赤松集成材 □105×105

3 10

斜梁：赤松集成材 □105×150

タープ：農業用ネット

手摺：Stパイプ Φ38
落下防止ネット

M12アイナット
ワイヤー Φ3
ターンバックル

700

1100

1450

550

FL (D2) = GL +3895

床：ヒノキ □45×105

FL (D4) = GL +3375

植木梁：スギCLT t90

Stパイプ Φ31

FL (E1) = GL +145

床：ヒノキ □45×105

床：ヒノキ □45×105

FL (C2) = GL +975

柱脚部：ヒノキ □45×45 ほぞ差込

梁：赤松集成材 □105×210

GL+131

GL+146

13

▼GL±0（設計GL

1800   1800   1800

⑪   ⑬   ⑮   s=1:25 detailed section

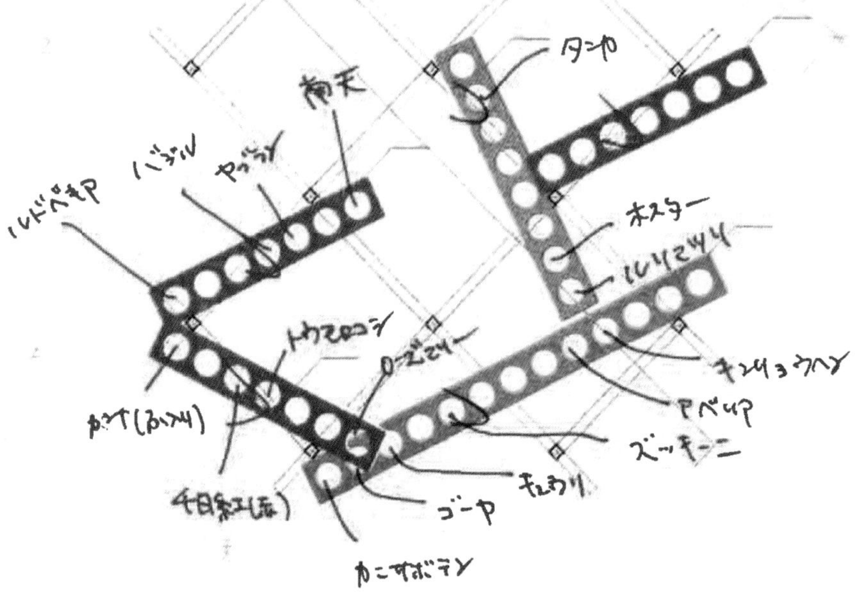

ハイビスカスP
バジル
ヤグラ
南天
タニク
アスター
ルリマツリ
キンリョウヘン
アベリア
ズッキーニ
キュウリ
ゴーヤ
かこすボテン
千日紅(赤)
カンナ(ふ入り)
トウモロコシ
ローズマリー

ベッパ
トウマンロウ
キンも...
マメツゲ
アサガオ
トウモロコシ
アガパンサス
カボチャ
トウガラシ
タニク
(ア)
ハイビスカス(赤)
アロエ
カンナ

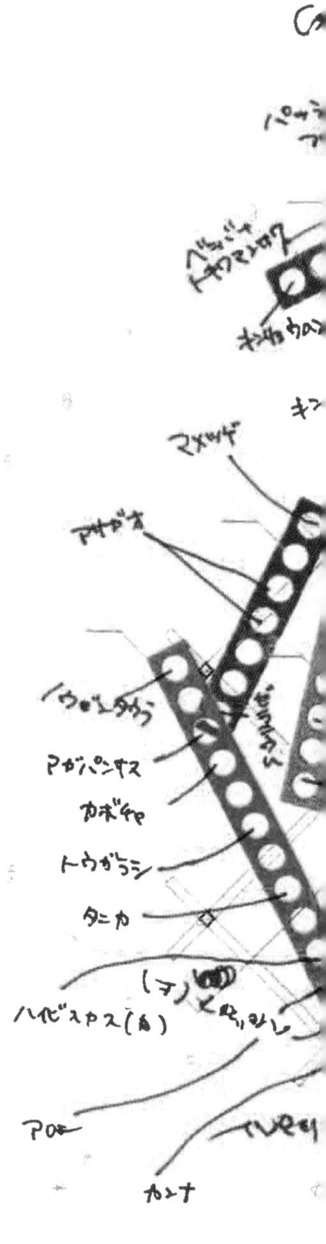

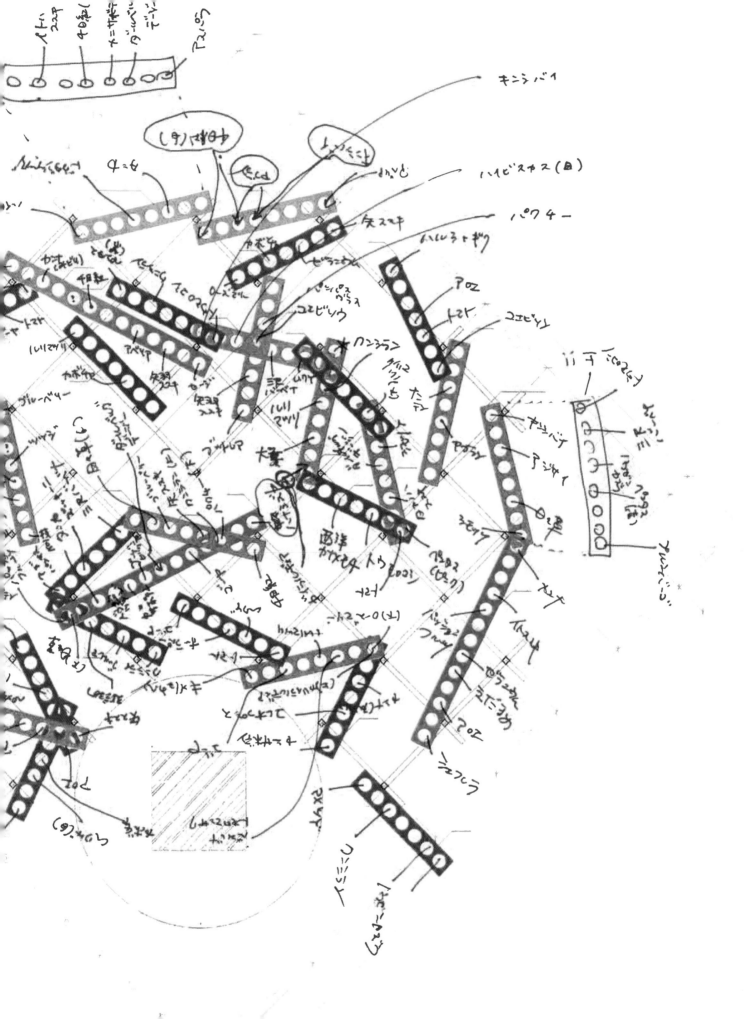

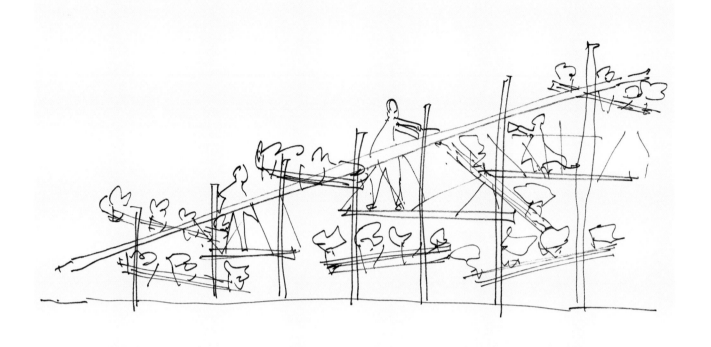

118

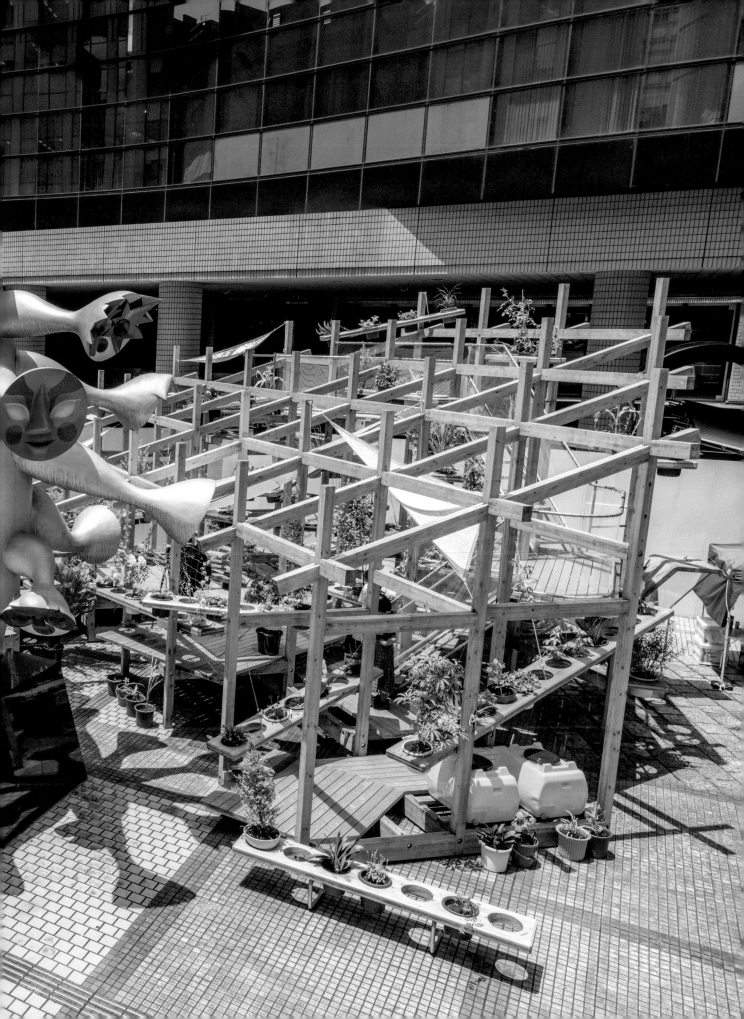

コンポストができるまで

ストリート ガーデン シアターの

写真・文章 寺内玲

用意するもの
★ 段ボール（二重構造のもの）
★ クラフトテープ
★ ピートモス ┐基材
★ くんたん ┘
★ スコップ
★ 段ボールの蓋になるもの
★ 段ボールを底上げするもの

作り方

（1）二重構造の段ボールを用意。二重でない場合は、自分で段ボールを切り貼りする。底は絶対に二重でないとダメ！

（2）段ボールの中にピートモス：くんたんを3：2の割合で入れ混ぜ合わせる、この総量が段ボールの7割くらいになるようにする。

くんたん：2
ピートモス：3

（3）段ボールごと、日当たりが適度に良くて風通しの良い場所に置く。下にレンガやカゴを置いて底上げし、風通しをよくする。

（4）真ん中にスコップで穴をあけ、野菜くずなどの生ゴミを入れる。その上に土を被せる。

○○を入れたところを中心に全体をか○。この作業は土に空気を合ませる○大事！これを毎日やる。

（6）虫除け、直射日光を避けるために、蓋をすると良い、いらないTシャツなどをかぶせてもO　あとは様子を見ながら（4）～（6）を繰り返す。

やすいものが良い。（ダメな例：玉ねぎ○○くくなったら米糠や廃油を入れる。基○

私たちは「ストリート ガーデン シアター」の制作の過程で、何度も東京の路上の園芸を観察に出かけた。道ごとに、家ごとに、植物の育て方、土、道具が異なり、それぞれに個別の歴史がある。東京という都市は、こうした路地庭によって自然と人工が織り交ざっているのだと思った。こうした路上園芸についての観察や考察を『ストリート ガーデン シアター ZINE』としてまとめた。「ストリート ガーデン シアター」というパビリオンは、建築をつくるというより、自然と建築を融け合わせ、東京という都市の園芸活動になる、というプロジェクトだったのだと思う。

In the process of creating the Street Garden Theater, we often went out to observe street gardening in Tokyo. Each street and each house has its own way of growing plants, using different soil and tools, with its own unique history. We realized that the natural and the artificial are interwoven through these street gardens in the city of Tokyo. These observations and thoughts on street gardening were compiled into the Street Garden Theater Zine. The Street Garden Theater pavilion was more of a project to blend nature and architecture into a horticultural activity for the city of Tokyo than to create architecture.

ストリート ガーデン シアター

2021年7月1日（木）から2021年9月5日（日）まで。こどもの城（〒150-0001 東京都渋谷区神宮前5丁目53-1）前にて開催。藤原徹平と仲間たちによってつくられる、植物と人間のための劇場。

東京城

会田誠

僕が新潟から上京した1984年はバブル期の真っただ中だった。
僕は繁栄のさなかにも、その正反対のものを幻視するような根暗な青年だった。
「新宿城」を作ったのは、まだ好景気の余韻が残る1995年。当時新宿駅西口にはホームレスたちのダンボールハウスが溢れていて、それを青島都知事が排除しようとしていた。

オリンピックが来るはずだった今年、若手建築家に混じって「パビリオン・トウキョウ」という屋外展に呼ばれた時、僕は25年前の「新宿城」を違う形で復活させようと思った。
ダンボールとブルーシート。この25年間に起きた、大震災や自然災害やオウム事件や原発事故や日本経済衰退に思いを馳せながら。
今は世界的にコロナ禍。
そして東京にいつかはまた来るだろう、決定的なカタストロフィ。
しかし仕方ない。
ポジティブ⇄ネガティブの往還にしか「力」は生まれないのだから。

「東京城」は逆説的かもしれないが、「健全でしなやかな力強さの象徴」として企画する。
2020年9月2日

以上は「生きている東京」展(ワタリウム美術館、2020年9月5日〜2021年1月31日)で「東京城」のマケット等を展示した際に壁に掲示したテキストである。以下もう少し補足しよう。

僕は恒久的なモニュメントや野外彫刻やパブリックアートにずっと懐疑的だった。
石やブロンズや鉄といった、古くからある固くて重いものであれ、FRPやステンレスを用いるジェフ・クーンズ[1]やダミアン・ハースト[2]などの現代美術系のものであれ。
しかし今回、矛盾した気持ちを抱えつつ、このイベントに参加することにした。
強調したいのは恒久性とは真逆の仮設性、頼りなさ、ヘナチョコさ ―― しかしそれに頑張って耐えている健気な姿である。どうなるか、やってみなければわからない。一か八か作ってみる。それを現在の日本 ―― 東京に捧げたい。

1. Jeff Koons、1955年〜。アメリカ合衆国の美術家。 2. Damien Hirst、1965年〜。イギリスの現代美術家。

Tokyo Castle

Makoto Aida

The year 1984 was at the height of the bubble economy when I came to Tokyo from Niigata. I was a gloomy young man who, even in the midst of prosperity, had fantasized about the exact opposite.
I made "Shinjuku Castle" in 1995, when the aftereffect of the economic boom still lingered. At that time, the area around the west exit of Shinjuku station was filled with cardboard houses of homeless people, and Tokyo Governor Aoshima was trying to get rid of them.

This year, just as the Olympics were scheduled to take place in Japan, I, along with other young architects, was invited to participate in an outdoor exhibition called Pavilion Tokyo, and decided to revive the "Shinjuku Castle" from twenty-five years ago in a different form.

Cardboard and blue construction tarps.
My mind wanders back to the great earthquakes, natural disasters, the Aum Affair, the nuclear accident, and the decline of the Japanese economy over the past twenty-five years.
Now, the global COVID-19 disaster.
And one day, Tokyo will face another ultimate catastrophe.
But it cannot be helped.
Because the "power" can only be generated through the alternation between the positive and the negative.

"Tokyo Castle" is planned, perhaps paradoxically, as a symbol of "sound and resilient strength."
September 2, 2020

The above text was posted on the wall of the "Living Tokyo" exhibition (WATARI-UM, The Watari Museum of Contemporary Art, September 5, 2020 – January 31, 2021) where a maquette of the "Tokyo Castle" and other works were displayed. I would like to add a few more words as follows.

I have always been skeptical of any permanent monuments, outdoor sculptures, or public art.
Be it an old, hard, and heavy object of stone, bronze, or iron, or a contemporary artwork like Jeff Koons or Damian Hirst using FRP or stainless steel.
This time, however, I decided to participate in this event despite my mixed feelings.
What I want to emphasize is the opposite of permanence: the temporality, insecurity, and vulnerability — and yet how hard one tries to endure hardships. You never know until you give it a try. I dedicate this work to Japan today — to Tokyo.

1. Jeff Koons 1955 – American artist. 2. Damien Hirst 1965 – British contemporary artist.

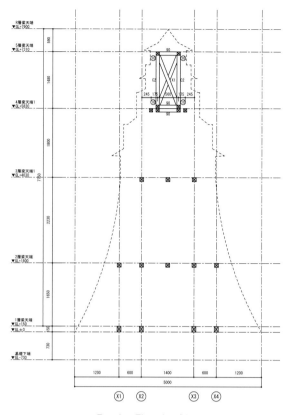

Framing Elevation (Y2+1,155mm)

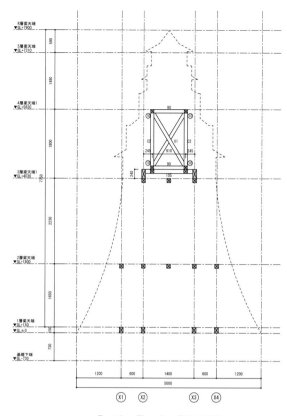

Framing Elevation (Y2+1,455mm)

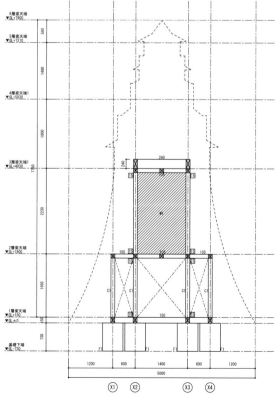

Y3 Flaming Elevation

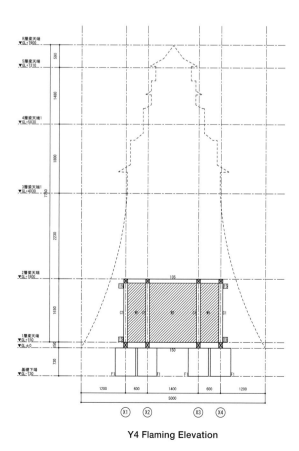

Y4 Flaming Elevation

会田 誠 2019

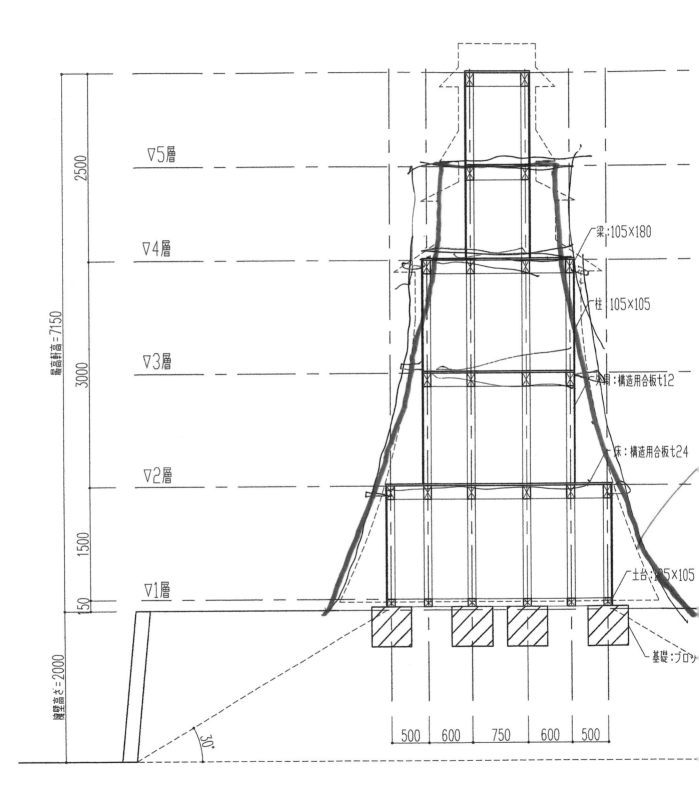

▽5層

▽4層

▽3層

▽2層

▽1層

最高軒高＝7150

擁壁高さ＝2000

2500

3000

1500

150

30°

梁：105×180

柱：105×105

壁用：構造用合板t12

床：構造用合板t24

土台：105×105

基礎：ブロッ

500 600 750 600 500

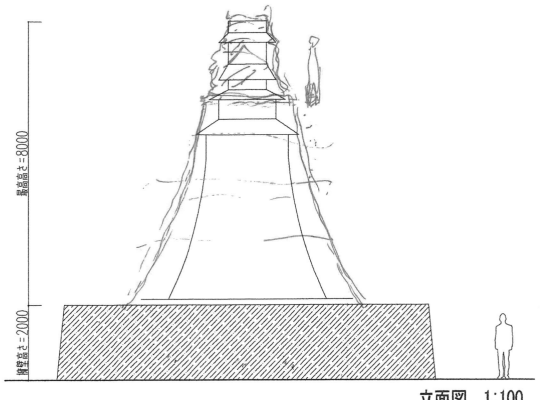

立面図　1:100

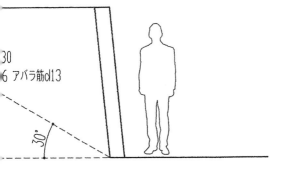

138

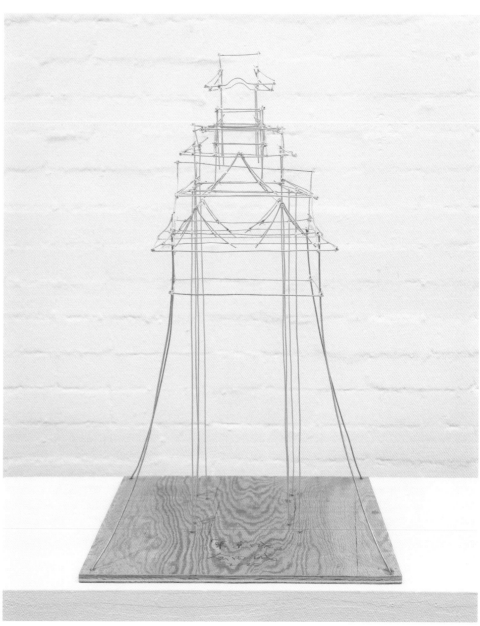

オブリタレーションルーム

草間彌生

The Obliteration Room

Yayoi Kusama

たとえば、身体じゅうに水玉をつける。それから、バックもすべて水玉模様にしてしまう。それがセルフ・オブリタレーション（自己消滅）。あるいは、馬に水玉をいっぱいつけて、バックも水玉にすると、馬のフォルムが消えて水玉と同化してしまう。馬の塊が永遠なものに同化していく。そうすると、私自身もオブリタレイトする。
（草間彌生『無限の網—草間彌生自伝』、2002年より）

For example, by covering my entire body with polka dots, and then covering the background with polka dots as well, I find self-obliteration. Or I stick polka dots all over a horse standing before a polka-dot background, and the form of the horse disappears, assimilated into the dots. The mass that is 'horse' is absorbed into something timeless. And when that happens, I too am obliterated.
(Yayoi Kusama, translated by Ralph McCarthy, "Infinite Net: The Autobiography of Yayoi Kusama," 2002)

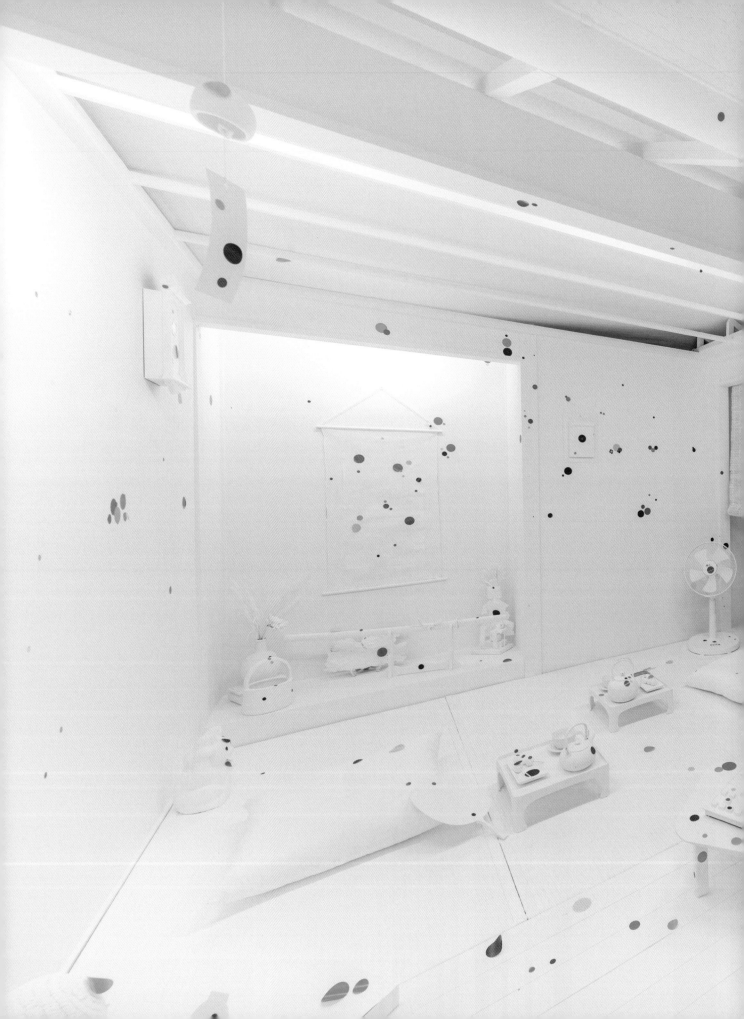

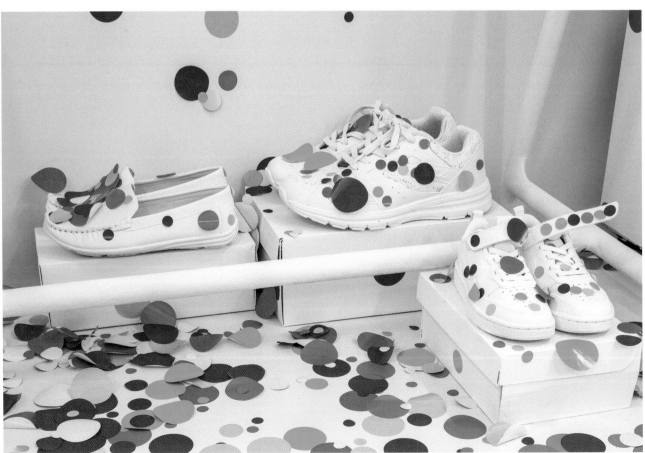

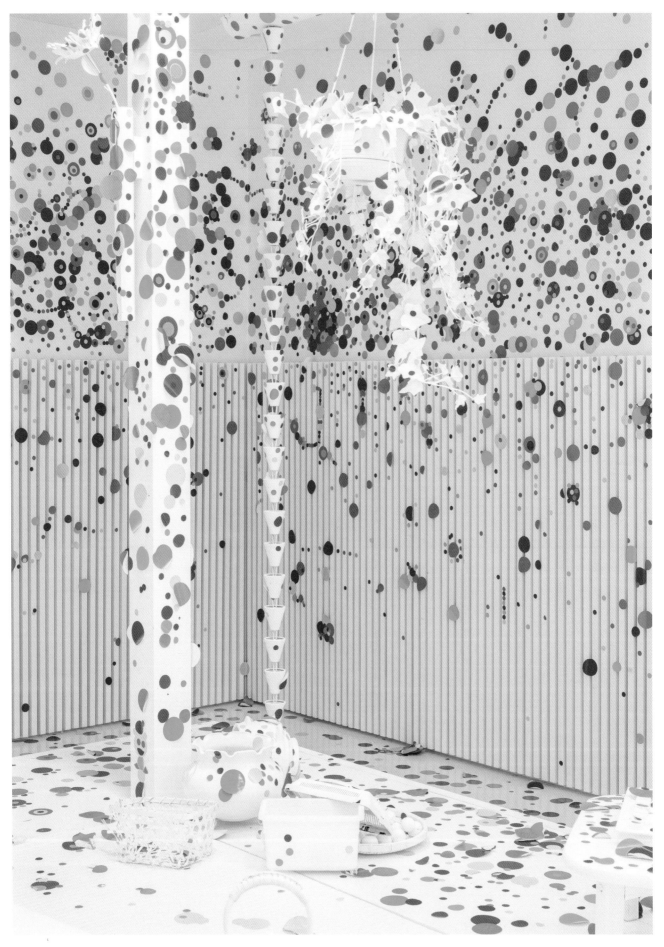

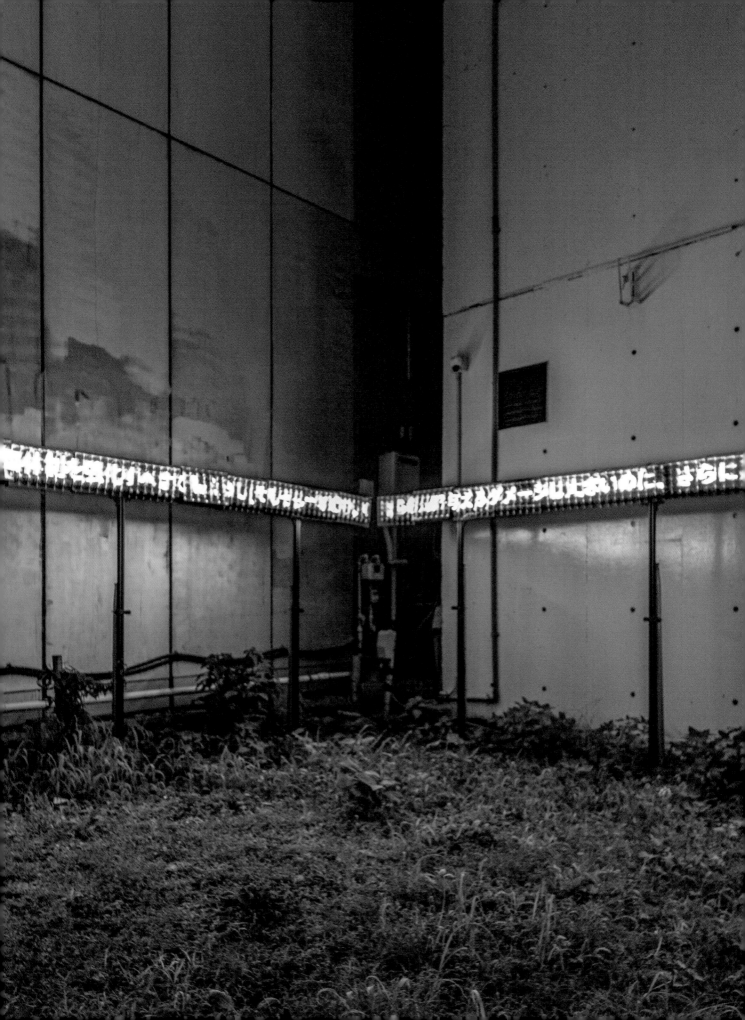

"2020-2021"

真鍋大度＋Rhizomatiks

"2020-2021"

Daito Manabe＋Rhizomatiks

この作品では、もうひとつの東京2020を展示します。2020年春の最初の緊急事態宣言から現在までに収集したさまざまなデータを使用して、AIが生成する狂喜乱舞する東京の姿。本来使用されるはずだったデータや中止になったイベントに関する情報などの特徴を抽出し、抽象化して文字や映像に変換し続けます。それらはディスプレイに光となって表示されますが、人びとが目にすることができるのはそれらの幻影です。

This work presents another Tokyo 2020, a frenzied state of Tokyo generated by AI using data collected since the first State of Emergency Declaration in the spring of 2020 to the present. It extracts and abstracts unique properties of data that were originally intended to be used and information about canceled events, and continuously converts them into texts and video images. These are shown as lights on the display, but what people see are their illusions.

パビリオン・トウキョウ 2021 展 at ワタリウム美術館

"PAVILION TOKYO 2021 exhibition at WATARI-UM"

「パビリオン・トウキョウ2021」開催中、制作の裏側をまとめた展覧会を開催した。クリエイターのうち7名の、制作時のスケッチや図面、模型、実際に使用された素材などを展示し、屋外で実際のパビリオンを体験した後、あるいはその前に、制作プロセスや詳細をより深く知り、楽しんでもらうための試みだった。映像作家・柿本ケンサクによる、施工プロセスとインタビューの特別映像では、それぞれのクリエイターが今の東京に対してどのような想いを抱き、パビリオンで表現したのかが語られた。また、展示したクリエイターのこれまでの活動や作品を切り口に、独自の視点で日本の現代建築史を捉えようと制作した「特別年表」も展示した。

While the "Pavilion Tokyo 2021," an exhibition showcasing the process behind the making of the pavilions was held. The exhibition, featuring sketches, drawings, models, and actual materials used to create the pavilions by the seven creators, was intended to provide visitors an opportunity to learn more about and enjoy the creation process and details of the pavilions before or after experiencing the actual pavilions outside. In the special video of the construction process and interviews by filmmaker Kensaku Kakimoto, the creators talked about their thoughts on today's Tokyo and how they expressed them through the pavilions. Also on display was a "special timeline" created to show the history of contemporary architecture in Japan from a unique perspective, drawing on past activities and works of the exhibitors as a starting point.

妹島和世 Kazuyo Sejima
水明 Suimei

藤原徹平 Teppei Fujiwara
ストリート ガーデン シアター
STREET GARDEN THEATER

藤森照信 Terunobu Fujimori
茶室「五庵」 Tea House "Go-an"

ランドスケープからの「パビリオン・トウキョウ2021」とアート

パビリオン・トウキョウ2021 実行委員　進士五十八（造園家）

若かりし頃、『緑の東京史』（思考社、1979年）を上梓するなどした私には、「武蔵野」といい、またよく「江戸東京」と呼ばれてきたように、TOKYOはどんなに超高層化が進み世界都市ランキング第3位と言われても、ひと皮めくれば土地のそこここに武蔵国や江戸的歴史風土に展開していることを痛感する。

それは今、「2021東京オリンピック・パラリンピックに向けた大東京大再開発ムーブメント」においてさえも変わらない。一見、無関係のようだが「パビリオン・トウキョウ2021」の作家らの場所選びに、それへの鋭敏さが見て取れる。これこそ「ランドスケープの力」というものだ。Landは土地・自然、scapeは全体・総合。東京を建物の集積としてだけではなく、地形、水系、緑地など、大地上に歴史的に展開する人間活動の総体が「美しい東京」を創出すると考えるからである。

江戸東京の場所性を生かし、巨大都市TOKYOの課題を告発するアート

「パビリオン・トウキョウ2021」は、現代日本の最前線で活躍しているクリエイター諸氏の関心事、問題意識、その上での大東京を見つめる眼力が美事に表出、作品化していた。その点で、実に鋭い都市文明批評になっていると思う。

もちろん、東京都生活文化局の支援等で実現した「東京オリパラ協賛のアートイベント」であり、クリエイターらは上品なユーモアで包んでいるが、深読みすれば大東京の課題を提示している。新型コロナウイルス感染症対策に圧し潰され、広く「東京は如何にあるべきか？」の都民的論議にならなかったのが惜しまれてならない。

聖徳記念絵画館の正面で、日本の現在を認識させる会田誠の「東京城」

象徴的な作品は、神宮外苑の聖徳記念絵画館へのビスタ、イチョウの4列並木の入り口、外苑のゲートに当たる左右石垣上の会田誠の「東京城」。この場所、この位置ならではの作品だ。周知のように明治神宮造営は、社殿と林苑の内苑は国費と各地からの献木と日本中の青年団員らの労働奉仕によるし、外苑は明治天皇顕彰事業への国民的寄付により、以後、国民的スポーツのメッカとみなされている。多くの人びとは、外苑を運動公園だと感じていたり、ザハ・ハディド案からウッドファーストの隈研吾案へと変わったものの、国立競技場用地と錯覚している。本来、大正期の国民的寄付による神宮内外苑一体の100年の「歴史的オープンスペース」であることを忘れないでほしい。

近代日本をつくった明治のランドマークの真正面に、ふたつの天守閣。ブルーシートは、異常気象下の災害列島と農村の今、またダンボールは格差社会東京のホームレスの今の象徴だと、私には映る。

アートシーンの創造力と推進力で魅力ある世界都市を目指す

「パビリオン・トウキョウ2021」の狙いが、東京オリパラ来場のインバウンドにフォーカスがしぼられていたようで、建築家、アーティストらは、"日本の伝統からの発想"と、これに"ふさわしい場所性"を見極めようと苦労されたようだ。大都市の大開発が進む現代東京では、場所を読む力を求められるし、その場所でのパフォーマンスを認めさせる粘り強い交渉力が、ワタリウム美術館など実行委員会には不可欠だ。ただ、これからの世界都市、コンテンポラリー・アートを楽し

める東京の魅力アップには、都市行政・観光行政の観点から、フィルムシティ並みにパブリックスペースの自由度を裁量する判断力が強く求められる。

極小の茶室が、極大のメインスタジアムを生け捕る藤森照信の奇想

今さら藤森照信作品の奇想独想深想に驚くことはない、と思いつつ、私は2階建て芝貼り茶室「五庵」に登楼。床の間の掛け軸代わりか、2方向に開かれた障子窓には巨大すぎると批判されてきた隈研吾設計の国立競技場がスッポリと生け捕られているではないか。

　日本庭園の借景手法では仰角10度ぐらいの対象をフレーミングするのだが、競技場前交差点の反対、ビクタースタジオ前をよく見つけたものである。ともあれ縮み志向の日本の空間文化・茶室で、巨大批判のスタジアムをかわいい景色に納めてしまう藤森先生の創作力には、脱帽するしかない。

妹島和世の現代版の曲水、特別名勝浜離宮恩賜庭園のパビリオン「水明」

曲水宴は、中国由来だが奈良・平安時代庭園の宴遊の景である。浜の御苑は江戸湾に突出して営まれた将軍家の庭。白帆輝く品川の海の向こうに富士を遠望する最良の視点場であった。海を埋め立てて造園した汐入りの庭を特徴とするので、およそ曲水は無理な場所。それを妹島和世氏は"水景"の力で汐留再開発ビル群と歴史的名園を共生させようと表現している。その思いが、文化財行政の堅固な氷を解かした。もちろん、埋蔵物保護のための制限をクリアするための技術的努力は、大変であったろう。

　渇いた巨大都市にとって、水系や水景がいかに重要かを、清らかで美しくやさしい作品「水明」を観た人びとは心に滲みて実感しただろう。

オープンスペースの本質を実感させてくれる藤本壮介の「Cloud pavilion」

東京都心で本物のオープンスペースと呼べる公園が、72haの神宮林苑と一体化した54haの代々木森林公園。そこに藤本壮介の「Cloud pavilion（雲のパビリオン）」。藤本は「雲はすべてを包む究極の建築」と言うが、正に多様性と寛容性をもち得る場所こそが、Open Spaceの本質だ。

　藤本作品は、近代東京が江戸以来のオープンスペースを喰いつぶしてきたことを再確認し、自覚もさせてくれるし、大東京にこそ緑と青空が不可欠だと教えてくれる。

藤原徹平の「ストリート ガーデン シアター」が、東京に江戸の植木・園芸文化を復活

江戸下町の縁日では植木市が立ち、狭い町家には下げ木の庭が、また、路地には魚河岸のトロ箱に土を入れ、ネギや朝顔、ホオズキなど草花を栽培した通り庭。身近に緑を求める庶民には、園芸趣味がささやかな楽しみだったのだ。

　藤原徹平はこうした江戸市民の緑のレガシーを、高層過密の無機的環境の中に再生しようとする。藤原氏の植木梁と称する木組みのジャングルジムならぬ立体構造体のある道広場は、明日からでも東京中の街角に調えられてよい楽しい試みだろう。

紙面の関係で触れられないが、国連大学前の平田晃久の「Global Bowl」は、最新技術を駆使した木材の3次元カットによる整形ボウルだし、石上純也の「木陰雲」は、エイジングの美を追求すべく、史的木造住宅の樹齢美豊かな庭内を雲形の焼き杉材で覆い、木洩れ日で自然の時と風景を醸成する。隈氏を含め、皆がウッドファースト。ここにも江戸のランドスケープに通底する心情を読み取ることができる。

　どうも本能的にクリエイターの皆さんは、現在進行中の巨大都市の生き方には、疑問符を付けているかのよう。草間彌生の「オブリタレーションルーム」の白い部屋で、私も何色もの水玉を貼ったが、われわれ市民はセルフ・オブリタレーション（自己消滅）するしかないのだろうか。

Pavilion Tokyo and Art from the Perspective of Landscape

Isoya Shinji (Landscape architect), Pavilion Tokyo 2021 Executive Committee Member

Tokyo, often called "Musashino" or "Edo Tokyo", is now surrounded by skyscrapers and ranks third in the world city rankings. Still, as the author of Midori no Tokyo-shi ("History of Green Tokyo," Shikousha, 1979) published in my early years, I am keenly aware that if you peel back the layers of the land, you will find the historical climate of Musashi-no-kuni (a pre-modern province encompassing present-day Saitama, Kanagawa, and Tokyo) and Edo unfolding here and there.

This has not changed even in the midst of the major Tokyo redevelopment for the 2020 Tokyo Olympics and Paralympics. While it may seem irrelevant at first glance, the creators of "Pavilion Tokyo 2021" demonstrated their keen awareness of this fact in choosing their locations. This is the power of landscape, where "land" refers to the land and nature, and "scape" refers to the whole and synthesis. This is because we believe that we can create a "beautiful Tokyo" by thinking about the city not only as an accumulation of buildings, but also as a synthesis of human activities that have historically unfolded on the land, whether it be topography, water systems, or green spaces.

Art That Makes Use of the Local Characteristics of Edo-Tokyo to Expose the Challenges of the Megalopolis Tokyo

The works of Pavilion Tokyo 2021 beautifully expressed the concerns and awareness of various issues of the creators who are at the forefront of contemporary Japan, and their keen observation of the great city of Tokyo. In this respect, I believe it presented a very sharp critique of urban civilization.

Needless to say, this was an "art event sponsored by the Tokyo Olympics" and made possible by the support of the Bureau of Life and Culture, Tokyo Metropolitan Government. While the creators cloaked this event in a sophisticated sense of humor, a deeper reading suggests that it presented challenges that Tokyo is facing. It was regrettable that a debate on what action Tokyo should have taken was not widely discussed by the citizens of Tokyo as the metropolis was overwhelmed by the measures to combat the COVID-19 pandemic.

In front of the Meiji Memorial Picture Gallery, Makoto Aida's "Tokyo Castle" Made Us Aware of the Present State of Japan

Makoto Aida's symbolic work, "Tokyo Castle," at the entrance to the avenue lined with four rows of ginkgo trees offer a vista to the Meiji Memorial Picture Gallery on top of the stone walls on both sides that serve as a gate to Jingu Gaien. This artwork was only possible in this place, in this location. As is well known, the construction of Meiji Jingu Shrine and the inner garden were made possible with government funds, wood donated from across the country, and volunteer labor from youth groups nationwide, while the outer garden was made possible by public donations to the project to honor Emperor Meiji and has since been regarded as a mecca for national sports. Many people seem to perceive the Gaien as an athletic park or mistakenly assume that it is the site for the National Stadium, which has changed from Zaha Hadid's proposal to Kengo Kuma's "wood first" proposal, but we should remember that the Jingu Inner and Outer Gardens are essentially a "historic open space" with 100 years of history, built with national donations during the Taisho era.

The two castles are placed directly in front of the landmark of the Meiji era, the period when modern Japan was founded. It seemed to me that the blue construction tarp symbolized the current state of the disaster-stricken Japanese archipelago and farming villages under abnormal weather conditions, and the cardboard symbolized the current state of the homeless in the disparate society of Tokyo.

Toward an Attractive Global City Through Creativity and Driving Force of the Art Scene

Apparently, Pavilion Tokyo 2021 was to focus on inbound visitors to the Tokyo Olympics, and the architects and artists struggled to find ideas drawn from Japanese tradition and an appropriate location for the pavilion. In today's Tokyo, where major urban developments are underway, the ability to have a clear reading of a place is necessary, and persistent negotiating skills for the actual realization of artwork in the place were essential for the executive committee including the Watari Museum of Contemporary Art.

However, in order to enhance the attractiveness of Tokyo as a world city where people can enjoy contemporary art, there is a strong need for urban and tourism administration to exercise discretion in the degree of freedom in public spaces on par with Film City.

Terunobu Fujimori's Extraordinary Idea of a Tiny Teahouse That Vividly Captures the Gigantic National Stadium

I went up to the two-story grass-roofed teahouse "Go-an," thinking that there is nothing to be surprised anymore by the strange, original, and profound ideas of Terunobu Fujimori's work. Shoji windows opened in two directions, perhaps as a substitute for a hanging scroll in the tokonoma (alcove), in which the National Stadium designed by Kengo Kuma, criticized for its overwhelming size, was perfectly captured.

In the "shakkei" (borrowed scenery) method of the Japanese gardens an object is usually framed at an upward viewing angle of about 10 degrees, and I was impressed to see that they had found this site in front of Victor Studio, diagonally across the intersection in front of the stadium. In any case, I have to take my hat off to Professor Fujimori for his creativity in the way he successfully captured the stadium criticized for its huge size into a charming view from the teahouse, a Japanese space culture oriented towards minimization.

Kazuyo Sejima's Contemporary Interpretation of Kyokusui: The Pavilion "Suimei" at the Hamarikyu Gardens, a Special Place of Scenic Beauty

Kyokusui-en, which originated in China, is a scenery for banquet in Nara and Heian period gardens. The gardens on the beach, jutting out into Edo Bay, belonged to the Shogun's family. It was the best vantage point from which to look out across the shining white sails on the sea of Shinagawa towards Mt. Fuji in the distance. Since the site was designed as a tidal garden created by reclaiming the sea, it was almost impossible to create kyokusui or a curved water feature there. However, Kazuyo Sejima used the power of waterscape to express the symbiosis between the Shiodome redevelopment buildings and the renowned historical gardens, and this idea melted the rigid ice of the cultural property administration. Needless to say, the technical efforts to clear the restrictions to protect the buried historical reserves must have been extremely arduous.

Those who saw Suimei, an unsullied, beautiful, and gentle work, must have felt in their hearts how important water systems and waterscapes are for a megacity suffering from thirst.

Sou Fujimoto's Cloud pavilion Lets Us Feel the True Nature of Open Space

Yoyogi Park, a 54-hectare park integrated with the 72-hectare Meiji Shrine Forest is the only park in central Tokyo that can be called an open space in the truest sense. This is where Sou Fujimoto's Cloud pavilion appeared. Fujimoto argues that "clouds are the ultimate architecture that encompasses everything," and an open space should essentially be a place for diversity and tolerance.

Fujimoto's work reaffirms and makes us aware that modern Tokyo has been eating up open spaces dating back to the Edo period, and that greenery and blue skies are vital to the metropolis of Tokyo.

Teppei Fujiwara's STREET GARDEN THEATER Brings Edo's Planting and Gardening Culture Back To Tokyo

There were plant markets at street fairs in "shitamachi" (downtown area of old Edo), and narrow townhouses had planted trees bought at the markets to make small gardens called "sageki no niwa." There were also street gardens in alleys where plants and flowers such as leeks, morning glories, and hōzuki (Chinese lantern plants) were grown in soils in trolley boxes from the fish market. Gardening was a hobby that gave a modest pleasure to the common people who wanted greenery in their daily life. Teppei Fujiwara aimed to recreate this green legacy of Edo citizens in the artificial environment overcrowded with high-rise buildings. Fujiwara's street plaza, with a three-dimensional structure resembling a wooden jungle gym which he calls a "planting beam," would be a delightful experiment that could be built on every street corner in Tokyo as soon as tomorrow.

While the limited number of pages prevents me from commenting further, I would like to touch on a few projects: Akihisa Hirata's Global Bowl in front of the United Nations University, which is a bowl constructed from 3D cut wood members using the latest technology, and Junya Ishigami's Kogage-gumo which attempts to pursue the beauty of aging by covering the garden of a historical wooden house with a cloud-like roof made of burnt cedar, generating a natural time and landscape with sunlight filtering through the trees. Everyone, including Kuma, seemed to embrace the idea of "wood first." Here too, it is possible to read the sentiments underlying the landscape of Edo.

Apparently, the creators instinctively question the ongoing way of life in the megacity. In the white chamber of Yayoi Kusama's "The Obliteration Room," I put polka dots of various colors in the space, wondering if we citizens have no choice but to self-obliterate.

反風景へのオマージュ

建畠哲（美術評論家・詩人）

パブリックアートといえば、まず思い浮かぶのは広場やホールなどの公共的な場所に設けられた彫刻や壁画などであるかもしれない。そこでは通常、不特定多数の人に抵抗感なく受け入れられる作品であること、都市空間を快適に演出するイメージであることが求められることになる。かつてのモニュメントはその場にまつわる歴史や物語を象徴的に体現するものであったが、今日ではむしろ特定の意味を排したニュートラルな造作であることが望まれているのである。

だがパブリックアートにはそうしたこととは別の、より本来的な役割があるはずである。美術館という専用施設に隔離されていたアートを現実の市民生活が営まれている場所に差し戻すこと。再開発などで歴史を奪われてしまった街の無難な装飾物としての役割に収まるのではなく、むしろそうした均質な都市空間のありようを変貌させ、時には挑発的に場所の意味やメッセージを復活させるもの。あえて言うなら街中から姿をくらましていた放蕩息子の帰還を意図するものではないか。

「パビリオン・トウキョウ2021」は、そうしたラディカルな試みを敢行するプロジェクトであるに違いない。参加したアーティストや建築家は、正直なところ、私には平穏な街に揺さぶりをかける桁外れの放蕩息子や娘たちのように思えてしまう。彼ら、彼女らが目論んでいるのは反風景であり、反建築であるのだ。しかし聡明なことに、このプロジェクトではそうした破天荒な試みを一方的に押し付けはしない。企画したのはこの街に生まれ育った方々で、地域の住民を説得する術に長けている。アーティストたちの大胆な振る舞いがテンポラリーなものであるならば、市民たちにはその挑発を受け入れるキャパシティーがある。親しんできた街の意想外の変容や不可思議な造作を、逸脱の風景として享受してくれるはずだということをよくわきまえているのだ。

たとえば会田誠氏の「東京城」である。神宮外苑の銀杏並木と青山通りが接するT字路には巨大な台座状の石塁がふたつ鎮座している。何も載っていない、あるべきものが

ない台座とは、不思議といえば不思議な都市の異物だが、会田氏はそれを「東京城」を支える石垣に見立てて、一方にはブルーシート製の、もう一方にはダンボール製の、壮麗にして珍妙でもある天守閣を築いてみせたのである。

ブルーシートやダンボールはかつて公園や地下街に出現し、見苦しいものとして撤去されてしまったホームレスの小屋を思わせずにはおくまい。仮設的な構築物とはいえ、雨風に耐える工夫をした城は、威風堂々とした姿を誇るだけに、作者の発想の途方もないユーモアをはらんだ批評精神をより強く印象付ける。それを近くの競技場で繰り広げられる国際的なスポーツの祭典へのゲートともいえる場所に据えるとは、なんともしたたかなアイロニーと言うべきであろう。

だが考えようによっては、それは極めて健全な発想でもあるのではないか。石やブロンズによるパブリックアートは、恒久的であることによってひとつの価値観、ひとつの美意識を市民に押し付けかねないが、設置者やアーティストにそんなことをする権利はないはずだ。公共の場所にアートを設置する方針には、いろいろな立場、さまざまな美意識を排除しない柔軟性や多様性が求められるのだが、テンポラリーであることはその条件にかなっており、たとえ自分の価値観や美意識とは異なった作品であっても、これはこれでいいんじゃないのと余裕をもって受け止めることができるのだ。「東京城」は仮設的であるからこそ臆面もなくアイロニカルな主張を掲げえたし、市民もまた突如出現したスリリングな反風景に対して寛容でありえたのである。

ビクタースタジオ前に設置された藤森照信氏の茶室「五庵」は、高い基壇をもつ不可思議な茶室である。藤森氏は草や樹木など自然を取り込んだ建築で知られるが、「五庵」でも基壇の外側は芝で覆われている。その上に載った黒々とした茶室の外壁には焼杉が用いられており、劣化を防ぐという条件をちゃんと整えている。基壇の内の暗闇は待ち合いで、そこから梯子で光に満ちた茶室に上がるという特異な仕掛けである。大きな窓から見えるのは、

完成したばかりの木を多用したオリンピックのメインスタジアム。茶会を開くならそれが軸物代わりの光景として話題にされるのだろうかというのはこちらの邪推で、自然体で生まれたアイデアが自ずと他に類例のない独創性につながっている藤森氏には多分そんな皮肉な意図はない。ともあれ、街中に挿入されたこんな異空間に一時身を置くことは、せわしない日常生活を送る都会人には何とも新鮮な体験であるに違いない。

　地図を片手にこうしたパビリオンを巡り歩くことは、見慣れているはずの街並みをスリリングな出合いの場に変容させてくれる。やがては消え去る光景だが、その記憶が次のプロジェクトへのモチベーションとなり、常に何かが起きる街としてのトウキョウの魅力につながっていってほしいものである。

Homage to Anti-landscape

Akira Tatehata (Art critic / Poet)

When we think of public art, the first thing that comes to mind may be sculptures and murals in public places such as squares and halls. In such places, it is required that the works should generally be accepted by a large number of people without offending them, and should enhance the pleasant atmosphere of urban spaces. In the past, monuments were intended to symbolically embody the history and stories associated with the place, whereas today, they are expected to be neutral creations devoid of any specific meaning.

However, public art has a different and more fundamental role to play. It is to bring back art, which has been isolated in the exclusive facilities of museums, to places where citizens actually live. Rather than merely serving as an harmless ornament for a city that has been deprived of its history by redevelopment and other means, it should transform the homogenous nature of urban space, and at times provocatively revive the meaning and message of the place. I would even venture to say that it is intended to be the return of the prodigal son, who had disappeared from the city.

Pavilion Tokyo 2021 is no doubt a project that dares to make such a radical attempt. Frankly speaking, the participating artists and architects seem to me like a group of outrageous prodigal sons and daughters trying to shake up a placid city. What they are aiming for are anti-landscape and anti-architecture. But the project is sensible enough not to impose such wild attempts unilaterally. The organizers are native to this city and are experienced in persuading local residents. They are well aware that if the artists' daring actions are temporary, the residents are capable of embracing their provocations, and enjoy the unexpected transformation of their familiar city and curious structures as a landscape of deviation.

One such example is Makoto Aida's Tokyo Castle. At the T-junction of the gingko tree-lined avenue and Aoyama Dori, there are two massive stone pedestals. The pedestals with nothing on top, or missing something that should have been there, exudes a foreign presence in the city. Aida used them as stone walls that support the Tokyo Castle, and built magnificent and curious castle towers, of which one is made of blue construction tarp and the other of cardboard.

The blue construction tarp and cardboard are reminiscent of the shacks of the homeless that once popped up in parks and underground malls, only to be removed as unsightly. The castle, a temporary structure that has been designed to withstand rain and wind, boasts a dignified appearance, which further highlights the critical spirit of the artist's idea filled with an extraordinary sense of humor. It was indeed a shrewd irony to place it at the gateway to the international sporting event at the nearby stadium.

But on second thought, this is perhaps a very sound idea. Public art made of stone or bronze may impose a certain value or aesthetics on the citizens by being permanent, but the installer or artist should not have the right to do so. The policy for installing art in public places requires flexibility and diversity that does not exclude various perspectives and aesthetic sense, and the temporary nature of the work meets this requirement. Even if the work contradicts one's own values and aesthetic sense, it can still be accepted with an open mind. The temporary nature of the Tokyo Castle allowed for unabashedly ironic statement, and the citizens of Tokyo were able to show tolerance towards the sudden appearance of a dramatic anti-landscape.

Terunobu Fujimori's Go-an, installed in front of Victor Studio, is a rather bizarre teahouse built on a high podium. Fujimori is known for his architecture incorporating natural elements including grass and trees, and in Go-an, the high podium is covered with grass on the outside. The jet-black exterior walls of the teahouse are made of burnt cedar, which properly meets the requirement of for preventing deterioration.

The dark space inside the podium is a waiting area, from which visitors climb a ladder to the light-filled tearoom upstairs. Through the large window, one is able to see the newly completed Olympic main stadium using lots of wood. It would be an unjustified assumption on our part to think that if a tea party were to be held there, the stadium would be the topic of conversation as a substitute for a scroll. Fujimori, whose spontaneous ideas naturally lead to unparalleled originality, probably has no such ironic intensions. In any case, it must be an extremely refreshing experience for city dwellers leading a fast-paced life to find themselves briefly in this otherworldly space inserted into the city.

The experience of walking around with a map in hand and visiting these pavilions transforms an otherwise familiar cityscape into a place of exciting encounters. While the scene will eventually disappear, I hope that the memories will serve as a motivation for the next project, and help enhance Tokyo's attraction as a city where new things are always happening.

東京は燃えていたか？

五十嵐太郎（建築史家・建築批評家）

東京オリンピック2020の閉会式において印象的だったのは、次回の会場となるパリへの引き継ぎ式の映像だった。エッフェル塔のまわりを旋回する飛行機から、トリコロールを示す3色のラインが空中に描かれ、巨大な旗が風になびく。そしてセーヌ川で開会式、コンコルド広場でスケートボードや3人制バスケ、グラン・パレでフェンシング、エッフェル塔でビーチバレー、シャン・ド・マルス公園で柔道、廃兵院でアーチェリー、ヴェルサイユ宮殿で近代五種などの競技を実施するという。100年ぶりのオリンピック開催に際して、名所を活用しつつ、都市の魅力を世界に向けてアピールしていた。もちろん、東京のオリンピックもそうした絶好の機会だったはずなのだが、あいにくのコロナ禍にみまわれ、開催の是非をめぐって賛否が分かれただけでなく、競技施設を無観客としたり、関連イベントも積極的に集客しづらいというダブルバインドの状況に置かれていた。こればかりは運が悪かったというほかはないだろう。

さて、これはオリンピック・パラリンピックを開催する国の義務でもあるのが、さまざまな文化プログラムが組まれ、特に公募事業「Tokyo Tokyo FESTIVAL スペシャル13」は大がかりなプロジェクトによって一時的に都市を飾った。これは場所の自由さや破格の予算などから、企画の募集段階から話題になったものである。例えば、現代芸術活動チームの目［mé］による作品「まさゆめ」は、実在する人の顔を巨大化させたバルーンを代々木公園や隅田公園の空に浮かべた。かくしてルドンの絵や伊藤潤二の漫画「首吊り気球」を想起させるシュールな風景が出現し、SNS上で話題となったが、現代社会の情報環境と相性が良い、都市型のプロジェクトである。また「東京大壁画」は、丸ビルと新丸ビルの壁面を巨大なキャンバスに見立て、横尾忠則と横尾美美の作品を展開した。これは新幹線のプラットフォームからもちらっと確認することができ、まさに東京の玄関口を意識したプロジェクトである。

「パビリオン・トウキョウ2021」も、スペシャル13の企画のひとつであり、都内の各地において建築家やアーティストが手がけた期間限定のパビリオンが登場した。建築家としては、世界的に活躍し、最高峰のプリツカー賞も受賞している妹島和世、ユニークな作品を発表する建築史家の藤森照信、そして新しい世代を代表する藤本壮介、平田晃久、石上純也、藤原徹平が参加している。国立競技場の仕切り直しコンペでは、最終的に隈研吾と伊東豊雄の2案の対決となったが、それぞれの建築家のスクールに連なるメンバーだろう。世界的に見ても、日本の建築界は系譜図を作成できるほど、次世代のすぐれた建築家が有名な事務所や研究室から続出する傾向が強いが、それを裏付けている。2025年の大阪万博では、藤本が大阪万博の会場デザインプロデューサーに就任し、その後、コンペによって伊東や平田の参加も決定した。2005年の愛知万博では、アトリエ系の若い建築家やアーティストが活躍する場が少なかったことを踏まえると、2度目の東京オリンピックと大阪万博は、一定の場を確保したと言える。

もっとも、「パビリオン・トウキョウ」で選ばれた建築家は、オリンピックの競技場や関連施設を担当してもおかしくない。レジェンドになった1964年の東京オリンピックでは、施設委員長を務めた岸田日出刀の采配によって、丹下健三、山田守、村田政真だけでなく、当時は40代だった芦原義信、清家清、30代の菊竹清訓らが設計に参加している。丹下ですら、オリンピックの開催時はまだ51歳だった。とすれば、ザハ・ハディドの国立競技場案をめぐるメディアの喧騒に目を奪われているうちに、他の施設は大きな会社の仕事になってしまい、今回は新しい個人の才能にチャンスを与えなかったのである。筆者は拙著『建築の東京』（みすず書房、2020年）で論じたように、東京の保守化がその原因ではないかと考えるが、せっかく現在の日本には優秀な建築家が多く存在するのに、単純にもったいないと思う。

ともあれ、こうした背景を考えると、本来はオリンピックの施設に関わるような建築家を起用した「パビリオン・トウキョウ」は、現状に対して、一矢報いたプロジェクトだったのではないか。

特筆すべきは、それぞれの持ち味を発揮しながら、自然の素材を用いたり、自然から着想を得たデザインが目立ったことだろう。例えば、妹島は真夏の浜離宮恩賜庭園において花を浮かべた涼しげな曲水、藤森は高い場所から国立競技場を眺めるための茶室、藤原は植木に注目した旧こどもの城前の「ストリート ガーデン シアター」である。また藤本は、究極の建築は雲ではないかと述べて、「すべての人のための屋根」としてあっけらかんとした「Cloud pavilion」を公園や駅に設置した。平田は、国連大学の前で3次元カットされた木材を複雑に組み合わせながら、身体に動物の感性を呼び覚ます「からまりしろ」の概念を実体化しつつ、もうひとつの小さなスタジアムとしてお椀の形状を与えた。そして石上の「木陰雲」は、九段下の近代洋風住宅の庭に対し、焼き杉でつくられた孔だらけの屋根をかぶせ、未来の遺跡のような風景を出現させている。ここは猛暑の日に訪れたが、まさに木陰が増幅されることで、本当に涼しい場所として過ごすことができた。

「パビリオン・トウキョウ」が興味深いのは、白い部屋にカラフルな水玉模様を与えた草間彌生など、アーティストも参加したことである。以前、筆者はChim↑Pomによる新宿歌舞伎町の解体予定のビルを使ったプロジェクトや会田誠の「GROUND NO PLAN」展（2018年）を論じたが、アート的な想像力は都市開発への批評的な視座をもちうるからだ（前掲書）。真鍋大度＋Rhizomatiksは本来、2020年に使われるはずだったデータやイベントの情報を加工しつつ、ワタリウム美術館向かいの空き地で流し、失われた「もうひとつの東京2020」を提示している。そして明治神宮外苑のいちょう並木入り口に登場した会田の「東京城」は、江戸城の石垣を転用した台座の上にダンボールやブルーシートを用いて制作された。これは1994年に新宿駅西口から撤去されたダンボールハウスの記憶を重ねつつ、「恒久的なモニュメント」への懐疑を表明したものである。わざと安価な素材で立派なお城のかたちをつくるというギャップ

ゆえに、脱力するというか、思わず、笑いを誘う。見方を変えれば、東京はハリボテになっていないか？　いや、安ければなんでもいい風潮への皮肉としても解釈できるかもしれない。笑いがもたらす破壊力は、多義的な方法によって東京を鼓舞する。

東京は燃えていたか？　どん底の経済状態にあった1970年代のイギリスにおいて、かつてパンクバンドのザ・クラッシュは、楽曲「London's Burning」（1977年）を発表し、「ロンドンは今、退屈で燃えている」と歌った。今回の東京オリンピックは、準備段階から開会式に至るまで立て続けに炎上し、無観客試合による異例の開催となった。「パビリオン・トウキョウ」は、そうした不発の国家イベントが進行する中で、小さな祝祭の火を灯したのである。

Tokyo Was Burning?

Taro Igarashi (Architectural historian and critic)

The most important part of the closing ceremony of the Tokyo 2020 Olympics was the footage of the Passing of the Baton Ceremony to Paris, the host city of the 2024 Olympics. Airplanes circling the Eiffel Tower drew tricolor lines in the air, and huge flags billowed in the wind. The opening ceremony will be held on the Seine, skateboarding and three-person basketball at the Place de la Concorde, fencing at the Grand Palais, beach volleyball at the Eifel Tower, judo at the Parc du Champ-de-Mars, archery at the Hotel National des Invalides, and modern pentathlon at the Palais de Versailles. In hosting the Olympics for the first time in a hundred years, the city was promoting its attraction to the world by making the best use of its famous landmarks. Of course, the Tokyo Olympics would have been the perfect opportunity to do so, but unfortunately, the COVID-19 pandemic placed Tokyo in a double bind situation: not only was the public divided over the pros and cons of holding the Games, it had to keep the Olympic facilities closed to the public, making it impossible to attract spectators to any related events. There was no other way to put it but to say it was bad luck.

As part of the responsibility of every country hosting the Olympic and Paralympic Games, a variety of cultural programs were organized, most notably the "Tokyo Tokyo Festival Special 13," an extensive open-call for public projects that temporarily graced the city. This program was highly controversial from the early stage of the call for proposals due to the discretion in choosing the location and the unusually large budget. For example, "Masayume," a work by the contemporary art team [mé], floated giant balloons depicting the faces of existing persons in the sky over Yoyogi Park and Sumida Park. The work generated surreal sceneries reminiscent of Redon's paintings and Junji Ito's manga "The Hanging Balloons", and created a buzz on social media. It was an urban project highly compatible with the information environment of today's society. "Tokyo Large Mural," created by Tadanori Yokoo and Mimi Yokoo, used the walls of the Marunouchi Building and the Shin-Marunouchi Building as gigantic canvases. This work, which could be glimpsed from the platform of the Shinkansen bullet train, was definitely designed with the gateway to Tokyo in mind.

Pavilion Tokyo 2021, one of the Special 13 projects, featured a series of pavilions created by architects and artists in various locations around Tokyo for a limited time.

Among the participating architects are Kazuyo Sejima, a globally acclaimed architect and winner of the prestigious Pritzker Prize, architectural historian Terunobu Fujimori who is known for his unique works, and representatives of the new generation including Sou Fujimoto, Akihisa Hirata, Junya Ishigami, and Teppei Fujiwara. The second round of the National Stadium design competition was ultimately a showdown between Kengo Kuma and Toyo Ito, and four of the six architects participating in this project are affiliated with either Ito or Kuma's school. From a global perspective, Japan's architectural world has a strong tendency to produce the next generation of outstanding architects from renowned architectural firms and studios to the point where it is possible to draw up a genealogical chart, and the selection of these architects underscores this tendency. For the 2025 Osaka Expo, Fujimoto was appointed as the producer of the venue design, and later, Ito and Hirata were also selected to participate through a competition. Given the fact that the 2005 Aichi Expo offered few opportunities for young atelier-based architects and artists, it is fair to say that the 2020 Tokyo Olympics and the 2025 Osaka Expo provided a number of opportunities for them.

It should be noted that the architects selected for Pavilion Tokyo were all competent enough to take charge of the Olympic stadium and related facilities. At the legendary 1964 Tokyo Olympics, architects including Kenzo Tange, Mamoru Yamada, and Masachika Murata, as well as Yoshinobu Ashihara and Kiyoshi Seike, who were in their 40's and Kiyonori Kikutake, who was in his 30's, participated in the design process under the leadership of Hideto Kishida, who served as chairman of the facilities committee. Even Tange was only 51 years old when the Olympics was held. However, this time around, while all eyes were on the media frenzy over Zaha Hadid's proposal for the National Stadium, the design of other facilities fell into the hands of big companies, and no opportunities were given to emerging talents as a result. As I argued in my book Kenchiku no Tokyo (Misuzu Shobo, 2020), I believe that this was a result of the growing conservativism of Tokyo. It is such a shame, given that there are so many excellent architects in Japan today. Against this backdrop, I believe that the Pavilion Tokyo project, which appointed architects who are competent enough to work on Olympic facilities, took a bold stand against the current situation. It is noteworthy that many of the designs used natural materials or drew inspiration from nature, while demonstrating unique characteristics of each designer. Sejima, for example, created a cool, flower-filled water feature called "kyokusui" at Hamarikyu Gardens in the height of summer; Fujimori, a teahouse for viewing the National Stadium from an elevated position; and Fujiwara, a "STREET GARDEN THEATER" in front of the former Children's Castle that focused on urban gardening. Fujimoto stated that the ultimate architecture would be clouds, and installed "Cloud pavilion" that serve as "roofs for all" at a park and a train station as a straightforward expression of this idea. By intricately combining three-dimensionally cut wood pieces in front of the United Nations University, Hirata materialized the concept of "karamarishiro" that evokes the sensibility of the animals in our bodies while giving it the shape of a bowl to express another stadium on a much smaller scale. Ishigami's "Kokage-gumo" covers the garden of a modern western-style house in Kudanshita with a perforated roof made of burnt cedar, creating a landscape that evokes a ruin in the future. I visited this place on an extremely hot day, and the amplified shade of the trees offered a truly cool place to spend time.

What was interesting about "Pavilion Tokyo" was the participation of artists including Yayoi Kusama, who rendered a white room with colorful polka dots. As I have discussed in the above mentioned book that referred to Chim↑Pom's project using a building to be demolished in Kabukicho and Makoto Aida's "GROUND NO PLAN" exhibition (2018), artistic imagination can offer critical perspectives on urban development. Daito Manabe + Rhizomatiks processed data and event information that was originally intended to be used in 2020, and played it in the vacant lot across from the Watari Museum of Contemporary Art, to present "another Tokyo 2020" that has been lost. Aida's Tokyo Castle, which appeared at the entrance to Icho Namiki, an avenue lined with ginkgo trees in Meiji Jingu Gaien, was created using cardboards and blue construction tarps on pedestals made of stones from the stone walls of old Edo Castle. This work expresses his skepticism about "permanent monuments" while overlapping his memory of the cardboard houses that were removed from the west exit of Shinjuku station in 1994. The way he deliberately used inexpensive materials to create the shape of a magnificent castle made me dumbfounded, or rather, laugh. Looking at it from a different perspective, could it be that Tokyo has become a papier-mâché city? Or perhaps, it could be interpreted as an irony against the trend of "anything goes as long as it's cheap." The destructive power of laughter inspires Tokyo in multiple ways.

Was Tokyo Burning? In the midst of the economic depression in the 1970's in the United Kingdom, the punk band The Clash released the song "London's Burning" (1977) and sang, "London's burnin' with boredom now." The Tokyo Olympics faced repeated backlash from the preparation stage to the opening ceremony, and resulted in an unprecedented event with no spectators at the games. In the midst of this unsuccessful national event, "Pavilion Tokyo" managed to light a glimmer of festivity in Tokyo.

あとがき「パビリオン・トウキョウ 2021」という企画の始まりについて

パビリオン・トウキョウ 2021 実行委員長　和多利恵津子（ワタリウム美術館館長）

事の始まりは1964年、私の東京オリンピック体験だった。私は小さい頃、北陸の小さな町で育ち、いつも裏山で駆け回っているような子どもだったが、小学2年生の春、父の仕事の都合で突然東京の代々木へと引っ越した。転校、大都会、オリンピックと大きな事件が続き、私はただオロオロしていた。ある時、参宮橋に向かう狭い道路の左側に新しく首都高速が登場し、近所の友達に誘われてよじ登ったことがあった。高速道路は開通前で、私たちはどこまでも走り続けた。「ここはとんでもなく都会で、未来はカッコよく、すぐに宇宙にだって行ける」。そんな興奮は私の東京体験そのものとなって、その後も長く記憶に残ることとなった。翌年、国立競技場近くの外苑西通り沿いに引っ越して以来現在まで私は、ここを拠点に変わりゆくこの街と人びとを見てきた。2017年、オリンピックが再び東京で開催されることを知り、なぜかあの未来都市経験が再びよみがえった。ちょっと恥ずかしいが、「パビリオン・トウキョウ2021」はそんなアニメ的な動機からだった。

めて1階の躙り口を潜ると、物語の街につながる。これは都市を生きる上で要となる体験だと私は思う。

　連日35℃を超える猛暑の中、側面の芝生には自動で水が循環するように仕掛けられていて、特に屋根のてっぺんの丸い帽子のような刈りこみが1度も枯れることがなかったのは見事だった（Fig. 1）。

Fig. 1　屋根の施工中、「五庵」から国立競技場を眺める藤森照信氏（2021年6月18日）。／Terunobu Fujimori looking out to the National Stadium from Go-an during the installation of the roof. June 18, 2021.

四畳半の茶室「五庵」と新国立競技場のツーショット

本企画のセンターポジションをお願いできるのは藤森照信氏の茶室しかないだろうと、企画当初から考えていた。本書の冒頭で隈研吾氏が「大きなものが終わって、小さなものが始まる」と書かれたことを私も痛感しており、日本最大規模の新国立競技場と対峙できるのは四畳半の茶室「五庵」しかないと考えた。梯子を登って2階の茶室に上がり、楕円形の大きな窓が巨大な競技場全体をすっぽりと飲み込んでいる様は、本企画の醍醐味のひとつとなった。

　藤森氏は「五庵」について、「芝生の丘の上に建つ灯籠です」と説明したが、私はさらに、時空を超えた世界をもっていると考えていた。現代的でも伝統的でもなく、強いていうならば宮崎駿の映画の世界のようだった。身体をすぼ

それにしても競技場のテロ対策と警備は相当に厳重だった。競技場周辺のほぼすべての敷地において、たった四畳半のスペースでも使用許可を得ることは至難の業で、この敷地の決定までには丸2年を要した。実現した音楽スタジオ前の駐車場は、私有地だがまさに最後の砦であった。

未来へとつながる水の流れ「水明」

妹島和世氏とは展覧会の会場デザインや、中南米への視察旅行でご一緒したことがあった。本企画では「真夏の屋外なので水を使うパビリオンはどうか」と私から提案させてもらった。妹島氏は、日本独自の美しさを絡ませることを考えておられた。剪定された松の木の姿に注目し、まずは皇居前広場の松林が候補に挙がった（Fig. 2）。しかし、皇居前は

オリンピックで競歩の会場となること、さらに使用許可には国会の審議と承認が必要であることから次の候補地を探すことになり、舞台は新橋の浜離宮恩賜庭園となった。浜離宮恩賜庭園は、東京湾の海水を引く潮入りの池や、鴨場を有する江戸時代の大名庭園で、25万㎡という広大な敷地をもつ。入り口前の砂利道や鴨場周辺など、いくつかの場所が検討された。形状も、噴水に始まり、さまざまな形の水路の案が出された。最終的に延遼館という明治時代の迎賓館の跡地が候補となった。現在は芝生が敷かれた敷地に、およそ3,000分の1の勾配で水を巡回させた。薄い木の土台に透明なアクリルを用い、深さ7mmの水路が111m続く。流れをコントロールするために、水の中には植物が配置された。透明な水の流れと周囲の超高層ビルとが相まって、時代を超えた新しい風景が誕生した。

Fig. 2　妹島和世、2019年7月頃の初期プラン。高さにより机にもベンチにもなる鏡面の板を配置した休憩所を、皇居前広場に提案。/ Kazuyo Sejima, initial plan around June 2019. Proposed a rest area in the plaza in front of the Imperial Palace featuring mirrored boards serving as either a table or a bench depending on the height.

設置にあたっては、地中に文化財の建物の一部が遺ることから地面の掘削や杭は一切厳禁、水の使用や工事の方法などさまざまな面で特例的な対応が求められた。妹島事務所の粘り強い対応と関係各位の尽力がなければ、この美しい風景は決して実現できなかった。

誇り高き「東京城」を決して忘れないだろう

異色のパビリオンとして話題となったのは、美術家である会田誠氏の「東京城」だが、こちらもスタート時は別のプランだった。高さ5mの赤い心臓を鐘楼に固定し、絵画館前の広場に設置するものだった（Fig. 3）。しかし、絵画館周辺はオリンピック期間中、選手のサブトラック（練習場）と

して使われるため、場所の変更を余儀なくされ「東京城」が浮上した。銀杏並木前の石垣の上を候補地として丁寧に描かれた会田氏のドローイングを見た時には思わず息をのみ、これは実現できるだろうかと自問した。場所、素材、テーマ、どれをとっても難問だった。建設局の占有許可、オリンピック・パラリンピック組織委員会の承認、港区の風致許可や景観条例、さらに素材の耐久性や構造、設置方法についても、入念なテストと確認が求められた。

ブルーシートとダンボールの作品は、災害国日本で被災した、多くの人びとへエールを贈ることを願いつくられた。また、一見やわに見える日本人が、底力を出して健気に立つ姿も連想させる。そんな会田氏のメッセージは、コロナ禍で元気のない東京を励ましたと思う。ダンボールでできた城が、雨にも負けず、会期中1日だけ降った大粒の雹にも負けず、ヨレヨレになりながら2か月間立ち続けた姿は誇らしかったし、東京という街の自由が少し広がったようで嬉しかった。このパビリオンは建築家には決して発せられない、人間臭い笑いと強さをもっていた。ほとんど毎晩、私は自転車でこの城を見に銀杏並木に出かけていた。

Fig. 3　会田誠、2018年12月頃の初期プラン。/ Makoto Aida, initial plan around December 2018.

2021年夏、9つのパビリオンが東京に現れた

藤本壮介氏は空の雲に建築の原点を感じ、長さ7.5mの雲を「Cloud pavilion」としてデザインした。設置した代々木公園とJR高輪ゲートウェイ駅構内には突如、不思

議な光景が現れた。青山通りの国連大学前、コンクリートの谷底のような広場に置かれた平田晃久氏のお椀のような彫刻「Global Bowl」は、子どもたちや近所の人たちで賑わった。その隣に設置された藤原徹平氏の「ストリート ガーデン シアター」は、植木鉢でできた物見塔。植物や、岡本太郎の彫刻「こどもの樹」、東京の街を上から「見る」という、普段とは違う視点を体験することができた。高層マンションに囲まれた日本庭園を、新たな光と影をつくることで見事に蘇らせた石上純也氏の「木陰雲」は、都市の新しい庭として人気のパビリオンだった。さらに日本を代表する芸術家、草間彌生の「オブリタレーションルーム」と真鍋大度のデジタル映像作品"2020-2021"が加わり、9つのパビリオンが輝いた夏だった。

敷地ごとの法規やルールにより、プランの修正が迫られる場面も多くあったが、クリエイターたちはさまざまなアイデアでそれらの課題を柔らかく乗り越え、作品をより豊かにした。例えば、「ストリート ガーデン シアター」は建築ではなく「物見塔」として設計することで、使用素材の制限が緩和され、木材を使うことができた。また、会田誠氏のブルーシート城へは色彩規制があったが、風対策用の土嚢袋に黒を用いるアイデアにより、乗り越えることができた。

クリエイターたちは通常、より良い作品をつくるために、完成直前まで時間のある限りプランをどんどん改善する。しかし設置にあたり事前の許可申請が必要だった今回は、細部にわたり原則数ヶ月前に申請した通りのものをつくらなければならない。申請先とクリエイター両者のギャップを埋めることが大変だった。われわれだけでなく東京都の担当者たちの尽力もあって進められた。

東京は再開発という名で知らないうちにどんどん変わっている。採算が合うものをつくるという経済性がこの街のすべての基準になった。しかし採算が合うとは一体どういう意味だろうか? 今こそ、金銭を目的としない場所、もの、ことが、どうしても必要な時代だと私は思う。今回設置したパビリオンは、短い間だったが、こんな場所が東京に存在するという既成事実となったと信じている。自慢したい大切な場所、生きる上で要となる場所、誰もがそんな場所をもつことができる、そんな東京がきっと実現できるはずである。

藤本壮介、2019年7月頃のプラン。高さ25mの「原始的な未来の塔」。代々木公園内に提案。/ Sou Fujimoto, initial plan around July 2019. A 25m-tall "primitive tower of the future." The proposed location was Yoyogi Park.

平田晃久、2019年7月頃の初期プラン。渦巻くように配置された材が、沸き立つエネルギーを表現する。渋谷駅前、ハチ公広場に提案。/ Akihisa Hirata, initial plan around July 2019. The swirling arrangement of members expresses surging energy. The proposed location was Hachiko Square in front of Shibuya station.

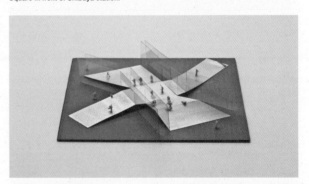

藤原徹平、2019年7月頃の初期プラン、コンセプト模型。出来事が偶発的に起こるストリートを劇場化し、明治神宮の鳥居前に提案。/ Teppei Fujiwara, concept model of the initial plan. The street where things happen by accident was turned into a theater. The proposed location was in front of the torii gate of Meiji Shrine.

石上純也、2019年12月頃の初期プラン。/ Junya Ishigami's initial plan around December 2019.

Afterword: On How the Pavilion Tokyo 2021 Project Began

Etsuko Watari (Director of WATARI-UM, The Watari Museum of Contemporary Art)
Chairperson of Executive Committee of Pavilion Tokyo 2021

It all started with my experience during the 1964 Tokyo Olympics. I grew up in a small town in the Hokuriku region in Japan, spending most of my childhood running around in the mountains behind my house. In the spring of my second year in elementary school, our family moved to Yoyogi, Tokyo all of a sudden due to my father's business. I was simply overwhelmed by a series of unfamiliar events: a new school, a big city, and the Olympics. A new Metropolitan expressway was built alongside the left side of the narrow road to Sangubashi, and I remember being invited by my friends in the neighborhood to climb it. The highway was not open yet, and we just kept running as far as we could. "This is a super-big city, the future is cool, and soon we will be traveling to space." The excitement of it all was the very essence of my Tokyo experience, and it remained in my memory for a long time afterwards. The following year, we moved to the area near the National Stadium along Gaien Nishi-dori, and I have been observing the changing city and its people from this base ever since. In 2017, I learned that the Olympics would be held in Tokyo once again, and somehow I felt compelled to bring back the futuristic city experience. It is slightly embarrassing, but I was driven by such anime-like, simplistic motive.

A Snapshot of the Duo: The Four-And-a-Half Tatami Teahouse "Go-an" and the National New Stadium

From the very beginning, we were convinced that Terunobu Fujimori's teahouse would be the best candidate to take up the central position for this project. At the beginning of this book, Kengo Kuma wrote that big things are over and small things are starting, which I deeply sympathized with, and I thought that the four-and-a-half-tatami teahouse "Go-an" would be the only one that could confront Japan's largest new National Stadium. Climbing up the ladder to the tearoom on the second floor and seeing the large oval window almost entirely engulfing the gigantic stadium became one of the best moments of the project.

Fujimori described Go-an as a "lantern on a grassy hill," but in my opinion, it has a world that transcends time and space. It is neither modern nor traditional, but rather like the world of Hayao Miyazaki films, if I may say so. Squatting down and crawling into the nijiriguchi (crawl-in entrance) on the first floor, you will find yourself in the city where the story unfolds. I believe that this is one of the key experiences for people living in cities.

Even in the heat wave of over 35 every day, the automated water circulation system on the grass on the side of the teahouse was functioning beautifully, and I was particularly impressed that the round hat-like topiary on top of the roof did not wither even once (Fig. 1). Security and anti-terrorism measures at the stadium were so strict that it was extremely difficult to get permission to use even a four and a half tatami mat (roughly 2.7m × 2.7m) space in almost all the sites around the stadium. It took us two whole years to decide on a site, and the parking lot in front of the music studio, which was privately owned, was our last resort.

Suimei, the Stream of Water Flowing into the Future

I have worked with Kazuyo Sejima on a number of occasions, including the design of an exhibition venue and an inspection tour to Latin America. For this project, I suggested to her the idea of a pavilion that uses water, given that it would be outdoors in the height of summer. Sejima was thinking of incorporating the unique aesthetics of Japan into her work. Noting the appearance of pruned pine trees, the pine forest in the plaza in front of the Imperial palace was first considered as a potential site for her work (Fig. 2). However, because the area in front of the Imperial Palace would be used as a venue for the walking race in the Olympics, and since permission for the use of the area required deliberation and approval by the Diet, we had to look for another candidate, and the stage was set at Hamarikyu Gardens in Shinbashi. Hamarikyu Gardens is a large garden of 250,000 that once belonged to the feudal lords during the Edo period, with a tidal pond that draws seawater in from Tokyo Bay and a duck pond. Various shapes of water features were proposed, starting with a fountain. In the end, the site of the former State Guest House from the Meiji period was chosen as the site for the project. The water was circulated at a gradient of approximately 1/3000 on the site, which is now covered with grass. The channel, made of transparent acrylic on a thin wooden base, is 7mm deep and extends

111m. Plants were placed in the water to control the flow. The transparent flow of water, combined with the surrounding skyscrapers, created a new landscape that transcends time.

The installation required special measures in various aspects, such as the use of water and construction methods, as excavation and piling of the ground was strictly prohibited due to the fact that, parts of the cultural heritage building remain buried underground. This beautiful scenery would not have been possible without the perseverance of Kazuyo Sejima and Associates and the efforts of all involved.

We Will Never Forget the Proud Tokyo Castle

One of the unique pavilions that attracted a lot of attention was the Tokyo Castle by artist Makoto Aida, which also had a different plan when it started. The first scheme was a 5m-high red heart fixed to the bell tower installed in the square in front of the Meiji Memorial Picture Gallery. However, given that the area around the Picture Gallery would be used as the sub-track (training ground) for the athletes during the Olympics, we were forced to change the location, and the idea of Tokyo Castle was born. When I saw Aida's meticulous drawing of the work standing on top of the stone walls in front of the Icho-namiki (gingko tree avenue) as a potential site, I was taken aback and asked myself if we could really make this happen. The location, materials, and the theme were all challenging. The project required occupancy permits from the Bureau of Construction, an approval from the Tokyo Organizing Committee of the Olympics and Paralympic Games, Minato Ward's scenic area permit and compliance with landscape ordinances, as well as careful testing and confirmation of the durability of materials, structure, and installation methods.

Aida's work made of blue construction tarp and corrugated cardboard was created in the hope of sending encouragement to the many people affected by the disasters in Japan. It also evokes the image of the Japanese people, who at first glance look frail and weak, exerting underlying strength and standing strong. I believe that Aida's message was a great inspiration to the people of Tokyo, who had been devastated by the COVID-19 pandemic. We were proud to see the cardboard castle standing there for two months, sagging, defying rain and even large drops of hail that fell for only one day during the exhibition, and I was happy to see that it seemed to help expand the freedom in the city of Tokyo. This pavilion had a humane sense of humor and strength that no architect could ever emanate. Almost every night, I would ride my bicycle out to the gingko tree avenue to go see this castle.

Nine Pavilions Appeared in Tokyo in the Summer of 2021

Sou Fujimoto felt the origin of architecture in the clouds in the sky, and designed a 7.5m-long cloud as the "Cloud pavilion." A strange scene suddenly appeared in Yoyogi Park and JR Takanawa Gateway station, where they were installed. Akihisa Hirata's bowl-like sculpture, Global Bowl, placed in a plaza that looked like the bottom of a concrete ravine in front of the United Nations University on Aoyama-dori, attracted a crowd of children and neighbors. Next to it was Teppei Fujiwara's STREET GARDEN THEATER which was a viewing tower made out of plant pots. There, viewers were able to experience a different perspective by "seeing" plants, Taro Okamoto's sculpture "Children's Tree," and the city of Tokyo from above. Junya Ishigami's Kokage-gumo, which brilliantly revitalized a Japanese garden surrounded by high-rise apartment buildings by creating new lights and shadows, was one of the most popular pavilions as a new urban garden. Also, with the addition of Yayoi Kusama's The Obliteration Room and Daito Manabe's digital video work "2020-2021", the nine pavilions sparkled throughout the summer.

There were many situations where the plans had to be revised due to the regulations and rules specific to each site, but the creators responded flexibly to the challenges with a variety of ideas to overcome them and enhance their works further. For example, the use of wood in the STREET GARDEN THEATER was made possible by designing it as a viewing tower rather than a building, thereby easing the restrictions on the materials used. In addition, Makoto Aida's blue tarp castle was subject to color restrictions, but he successfully solved this problem by using black sandbags for wind protection.

Creators usually continue to fine-tune their plans until the last minute to create a better work. This time, however, when we had to apply for a number of permits for the exhibition, we had to make sure that every detail was consistent with the plans we had submitted a few months before. It was a challenging task to bridge the gap between the parties involved in the process and the creators. But we were able to proceed with the project thanks to the efforts of the Tokyo Metropolitan Government officials as well as our own.

Tokyo is undergoing rapid changes in the name of redevelopment without us even knowing it. The idea of economy, of making things that are economically viable, has become the basis for everything in this city. But what does it mean to be economically viable? I believe that now is the time when we desperately need places, things, and experiences that are not about money. They are essential for human life. I believe that the pavilions, although they were set up for a short time, have established the fact that such places existed in Tokyo. I am convinced that we will be able to build an era in which everyone can have a place to be proud of, a place that is essential to life.

作家略歴

藤森照信

1946年生まれ。東京大学大学院工学系研究科博士課程修了。現在、江戸東京博物館館長、東京大学名誉教授、工学院大学特任教授。近代建築史・都市史研究を経て1991年、45歳の時に「神長官守矢史料館」で建築家としてデビュー。土地固有の自然素材を多用し、自然と人工物が一体となった姿の建物を多く手がけている。建築の工事には、素人で構成される「縄文建築団」が参加することも。代表作に「タンポポハウス」、「ニラハウス」、「高過庵」など。近作に「多治見市モザイクタイルミュージアム」や「ラ コリーナ近江八幡」の「草屋根」、「銅屋根」などがある。

妹島和世

1956年生まれ。日本女子大学大学院家政学部住居学科修了。1987年妹島和世建築設計事務所設立。1995年西沢立衛と共にSANAAを設立。代表作に「金沢21世紀美術館」、ニューヨークの「ニュー・ミュージアム」、「ルーヴル・ランス」、「すみだ北斎美術館」（妹島事務所として）、最新作「大阪芸術大学アートサイエンス学科棟」（妹島事務所として）など。2010年、第12回ヴェネチア・ビエンナーレ国際建築展にて、日本人、そして女性として初めて総合ディレクターを務める。プリツカー賞、ヴェネチア・ビエンナーレ国際建築展金獅子賞、日本建築学会賞、紫綬褒章（個人として）、他受賞多数。※上記の建築作品、受賞は特記のない限りSANAA名義。

藤本壮介

1971年生まれ。東京大学工学部建築学科卒業後、2000年に藤本壮介建築設計事務所を設立。主な作品に「武蔵野美術大学美術館・図書館」、ロンドンの「サーペンタイン・ギャラリー・パビリオン2013」、フランス・モンペリエの「L'Arbre Blanc」、最新作「白井屋ホテル」など。2014年フランス・モンペリエ国際設計競技最優秀賞、2015年パリ・サクレー・エコール・ポリテクニーク・ラーニングセンター国際設計競技最優秀賞につぎ、2016年Reinventer.paris国際設計競技ボルトマイヨ・パーシング地区最優秀賞を受賞。2025年日本国際博覧会（大阪・関西万博）の会場デザインプロデューサーを務める。

平田晃久

1971年生まれ。京都大学大学院工学研究科修了。伊東豊雄建築設計事務所を経て、2005年に平田晃久建築設計事務所を設立。現在、京都大学教授。主な作品に「Bloomberg Pavilion」、「Tree-ness House」、「太田市美術館・図書館」など。2022年に完成予定の「神宮前六丁目地区第一市街地再開発事業」の外装・屋上デザインを手がける。第19回JIA新人賞、Elita Design Award、第13回ヴェネチア・ビエンナーレ国際建築展金獅子賞（日本館）、日本建築設計学会賞、村野藤吾賞など受賞多数。2016年にニューヨーク近代美術館の「Japanese Constellation」展に参加。

石上純也

1974年生まれ。東京藝術大学大学院美術研究科建築専攻修士課程修了。妹島和世建築設計事務所を経て、2004年石上純也建築設計事務所を設立。東京理科大学非常勤講師、東北大学大学院特任准教授、2014年よりハーバード大学大学院客員教授を歴任。主な作品に「神奈川工科大学KAIT工房」、「アート・ビオトープ那須」の「水庭」、「サーペンタイン・ギャラリー・パビリオン2019」など。日本建築学会賞、第12回ヴェネチア・ビエンナーレ国際建築展金獅子賞など受賞多数。2018年、パリのカルティエ現代美術財団で大規模個展「石上純也 自由な建築」展を開催。

藤原徹平

1975年生まれ。横浜国立大学大学院工学研究科修士課程修了。2001年より隈研吾建築都市設計事務所にて、「ティファニー銀座」、「北京・三里屯SOHO」、「浅草文化観光センター」、「マルセイユ現代美術センター」など世界20都市以上のプロジェクトを担当。2009年よりフジワラテッペイアーキテクツラボ代表。2010年よりNPO法人ドリフターズインターナショナル理事。2012年より横浜国立大学大学院Y-GSA准教授。アートや演劇、都市など他分野に越境した活動を行っている。主な作品に「クルックフィールズ」、「那須塩原市まちなか交流センター くるる」、「稲村の森の家」、「リボーンアートフェスティバル2017会場デザイン」など。

会田誠

1965年生まれ。東京藝術大学大学院美術研究科修了（油画技法・材料研究室）。美少女、戦争、サラリーマンなど、社会や歴史、現代と近代以前、西洋と東洋の境界を自由に往来し、奇想天外な対比や痛烈な批評性を提示する作風で、幅広い世代から圧倒的な支持を得ている。平面作品に限らず、彫刻、パフォーマンス、映像、小説や漫画の執筆など活動は多岐にわたる。近年の主な個展に、「天才でごめんなさい」（2012-13年、森美術館）、「考えない人」（2014年、ブルターニュ公爵城（ナント、フランス））、「ま、Still Alive ってこーゆーこと」（2015年、新潟県立近代美術館）、「GROUND NO PLAN」（2018年、青山クリスタルビル）などがある。

草間彌生

1929年生まれ。幼少期から幻視・幻聴を体験し、水玉や網模様をモチーフに絵画を制作し始め、1957年単身渡米、単一モチーフの強迫的な反復と増殖による自己消滅という芸術哲学を見出し、ネット・ペインティング、ソフト・スカルプチャー、鏡や電飾を使った環境彫刻やハプニングなど多様な展開を見せ、前衛芸術家としての地位を確立。芸術活動の傍ら、小説、詩集も多数発表。代表作に「無限の網」「水玉強迫」「南瓜」「わが永遠の魂」などがある。現在も国内外で精力的に活動を続ける、最も重要な日本人アーティストのひとりである。2016年文化勲章を受章。2017年には、国立新美術館で大回顧展を開催。同年、「草間彌生美術館」を東京・新宿にオープン。

真鍋大度

アーティスト、プログラマ、DJ。2006年Rhizomatiks設立。身近な現象や素材を異なる目線で捉え直し、組み合わせることで作品を制作。高解像度、高臨場感といったリッチな表現を目指すのでなく、注意深く観察することにより発見できる現象、身体、プログラミング、コンピュータそのものがもつ本質的な面白さや、アナログとデジタル、リアルとバーチャルの関係性、境界線に着目し、さまざまな領域で活動している。

Profile

Terunobu Fujimori

Born in 1946. He got his phD from the University of Tokyo. Now he is a director of Edo Tokyo Museum, a professor emeritus of the University of Tokyo, and a professor of Kogakuin University. After a long career as a researcher of modern architectural history and urban history, he debuted as an architect with Jinchokan Moriya Historical Museum in 1991, when he was 45 years old. He creates architectures in which nature and artifacts integrate. "Team Jomon Architeture," consisted of amateurs, sometimes helps to construct his work. His representative works are Tanpopo House (Dandelion House), Nira House (Leek House), Takasugi-an Tea House, and more. Recently he completed Mosaictile-Museum Tajimi and Kusayane and Douyane in La Collina Omi-Hachiman.

Kazuyo Sejima

Born in 1956. She got her master's degree from Japan Women's University. She established Kazuyo Sejima & Associates in 1987 and SANAA with Ryue Nishizawa in 1995. She often uses acrylic and metal materials and makes space and people connecting loosely. Their representative works are 21st Century Museum of Contemporary Art, The New Museum of Contemporary Art in New York, Le Louvre-Lens, The Sumida Hokusai Museum (as Kazuyo Sejima & Associates) and her latest work Department of Art Science at Osaka University of Arts (as Kazuyo Sejima & Associates). In 2010, she was appointed director of architecture sector for the Venice Biennale as the first Japanese and female director. SANAA got many prizes including the AIJ Prize, the Golden Lion for the most remarkable work at the 12th Venice Biennale in 2004, the Pritzker Prize in 2010, and Sejima got Medal with Purple Ribbon in 2016.

Sou Fujimoto

Born in 1971. He started Sou Fujimoto Architects in 2000, soon after his graduation from the Faculty of Engineering at the University of Tokyo with a degree in architecture. His representative works are Musashino Art University Museum & Library, Serpentine Gallery Pavilion 2013 in London, L'Arbre Blanc in Montpellier, France, and his latest work SHIROIYA HOTEL. He was selected as a winner of several international competitions; the Ecole Polytechnique Learning Centre in Paris in 2015, and the Reinventing Paris project in Pershing/Porte Maillot in 2016. He is the Expo site design producer for the 2025 Japan International Exposition (Osaka/Kansai Expo).

Akihisa Hirata

Born in 1971. He got his master's degree from Kyoto University in 1997. After working for Toyo Ito & Associates, Architects, established his own office, Akihisa Hirata Architecture Office in 2005. Now he is a professor of Kyoto University. His representative works are Kotoriku, Art Museum & Library, Ota, and 9h nine hours. He is working on the exterior and rooftop design for the Jingumae 6-chome Urban Redevelopment Project, scheduled for completion in 2022. He got many prizes; the 19th JIA Newface Award, Elita Design Award (Photosynthesis), the Golden Lion at the 13th Venice Biennale in 2012 and more. He participated in an exhibition, Japanese Constellation in MoMA in 2016.

Junya Ishigami

Born in 1974. He acquired his master's degree in architecture and planning at Tokyo National University of Fine Arts and Music in 2000. After working in Kazuyo Sejima & Associates, he established his own firm in 2004: junya.ishigami+associates. He worked as a part time instructor at Tokyo University of Science, an associate professor at Tohoku University, and the Kenzo Tange Design Critic at the Harvard Graduate School of Design from 2014. His representative works are the Kanagawa Institute of Technology KAIT Workshop, Water Garden in Art Biotop Nasu, and Serpentine Gallery Pavilion 2019. He got many prizes; AIJ Prize for Architectural Design in 2009, and the Golden Lion for Best Project at the 12th Venice Architecture Biennale in 2010. He held a large-scale exhibition "Junya Ishigami, Freeing Architecture" in Foundation Cartier pour l'art contemporain in 2018.

Teppei Fujiwara

Born in 1975. He got his master degree from the Yokohama National University. Before he established his own firm, FUJIWALABO in 2009, he had worked in Kengo Kuma & Associates from 2001 and designed many projects in more than twenty cities in the world; Tiffany Ginza, Sanlitun Soho in Beijing, Asakusa Culture Tourist Information Center, FRAC Marseille, and more. He also acts as a director of a NPO Drifters International from 2010 and an assistant professor of Y-GSA at Yokohama National University from 2012. His practices cross the border between architecture and other fields including art, theater and urban scale matters. His representative works are KURKKU FIELDS, Nasushiobara Community Center Kururu, Inamura House and Gardens, and venue design for Reborn-Art Festival 2017.

Makoto Aida

Born in 1965. He got his master's degree in Fine Arts from the Tokyo National University of Fine Arts. He often uses pretty young girls, war and office workers as his motifs. He comes and goes freely between society and history, current time and pre-modern period, west and east and presents an unexpected contrast and a caustic criticism. He gains overwhelming support from people in all generation. He has a wide range of works not only paintings, but also sculpture, performance, films, novels and manga. His recent exhibitions are "Monument for Nothing" (Mori Art Museum, Tokyo, 2012), "Le Non-penseur (The Non-Thinker)" (Château des ducs de Bretagne, Nantes, France, 2014), "So, this is what they call 'Still Alive'" (Niigata Prefectural Museum of Modern Art, 2015), "GROUND NO PLAN" (Aoyama Crystal Building, Tokyo, 2018).

Yayoi Kusama

Born in 1929. She has experienced visions and auditory hallucinations from an early age, and began to draw polka dots and net patterns as motifs. In 1957, she moved to United States by herself and discovered an artistic philosophy of self-obliteration through obsessive repetition and multiplication of a single motif, and established herself as an avant-garde artist by developing a diverse range of works including net paintings, soft sculptures, environmental sculptures using mirrors and electric lights, and happenings. In addition to her artistic activities, she has also published a number of novels and poems. Her representative works include Infinity Net, Dots Obsession, Pumpkin, and My Eternal Soul. She is one of the most important Japanese artists, continuing to work energetically in and outside Japan today. In 2017, she held a large retrospective exhibition "My Eternal Soul" (The National Art Center, Tokyo) and in the same year, the Yayoi Kusama Museum opened in Shinjuku, Tokyo.

Daito Manabe

Artist, programmer, and DJ. Launched Rhizomatiks in 2006. Manabe's works, which range into a variety of fields, takes a new approach to everyday materials and phenomena. However, his end goal is not simply rich, high-definition realism by recognizing and recombining these familiar elemental building blocks. Rather, his practice is informed by careful observation to discover and elucidate the essential potentialities inherent to the human body, data, programming, computers, and other phenomena, thus probing the interrelationships and boundaries delineating the analog and digital, real and virtual.

「パビリオン・トウキョウ2021」企画クレジット

❙ Tokyo Tokyo FESTIVAL スペシャル13「パビリオン・トウキョウ2021」
開催期間：2021年7月1日（木）–9月5日（日）
会場：新国立競技場周辺エリアを中心に東京都内各所
パビリオン・クリエイター：藤森照信、妹島和世、藤本壮介、平田晃久、石上純也、藤原徹平、会田誠、草間彌生
特別参加：真鍋大度＋Rhizomatiks
主催：東京都、公益財団法人東京都歴史文化財団 アーツカウンシル東京、パビリオン・トウキョウ2021実行委員会
企画：ワタリウム美術館

❙ パビリオン・トウキョウ2021実行委員会
名誉実行委員長：隈研吾（建築家）
実行委員長：和多利恵津子（ワタリウム美術館館長）
実行委員：長谷部健（渋谷区長）、吉住健一（新宿区長）、武井雅昭（港区長）、進士五十八（福井県立大学学長、造園学者）、米倉誠一郎（経済学者）
制作委員長：和多利浩一（ワタリウム美術館CEO）
アートディレクター：groovisions
運営：アースガーデン /（有）en
クリエイターインタビュー、ガイドブック用地図制作、記録書籍出版：TOTO出版
法律担当：水野祐（シティライツ法律事務所 代表）
監事：佐々木誠（山岸睦夫税理士事務所）

❙ スポンサー
特別協賛：株式会社大林組 / 株式会社ジンズホールディングス
協賛：東邦レオ株式会社 / 株式会社エヌ・シー・エヌ / Cartier / エイベックス・ビジネス・ディベロップメント株式会社 / 株式会社FORM GIVING / 株式会社 中川ケミカル / 北京益汇达清水建筑工程有限公司 / 袁鑫工程顾问（上海）事务所 / 重庆纬图景观设计有限公司 / 株式会社JVCケンウッド・ビクターエンタテインメント / 株式会社ユニオン / 株式会社 資生堂 / 大成建設株式会社
カート協力・水提供：株式会社カクイチ
警備協力：後藤商店株式会社

❙ 藤森照信　茶室「五庵」
会場：ビクタースタジオ前（東京都渋谷区神宮前2-21-1）
茶室制作：川本英樹（川本家具製作研究所）
基壇実施設計：大嶋信道（大嶋アトリエ）
基壇施工：宮嶋孝秀（株式会社 宮嶋工務店）
緑化施工：大林武彦（株式会社 大林環境技術研究所）
茶室仕上げ材（銅板、焼き杉、漆喰）制作施工協力：工学院大学大内田史郎ゼミ

❙ 妹島和世「水明」
会場：浜離宮恩賜庭園 延遼館跡（東京都中央区浜離宮庭園）
施工協力：有限会社工藤工務店 / 有限会社オーツー / 株式会社クリック
素材協力：リンテックサインシステム株式会社

❙ 藤本壮介「Cloud pavilion（雲のパビリオン）」
第1会場：代々木公園パノラマ広場付近（東京都渋谷区代々木神園町、神南二丁目）
第2会場：高輪ゲートウェイ駅 改札内（東京都港区港南2-1-220）
会場協力：東日本旅客鉄道株式会社
施工協力：株式会社田中工務店
バルーン制作：有限会社クラウン・ビー
構造設計：東京藝術大学美術学部建築科教授 金田充弘＋株式会社テクトニカ

❙ 平田晃久「Global Bowl」
会場：国際連合大学前（東京都渋谷区神宮前5-53-70）
構造設計：東京藝術大学美術学部建築科教授　金田充弘
施工協力：株式会社シェルター
照明協力：大光電機株式会社

❙ 石上純也「木陰雲」
会場：kudan house庭園（東京都千代田区九段北1-15-9）
協賛：東邦レオ株式会社 / Cartier / 株式会社 中川ケミカル / 北京益汇达清水建筑工程有限公司 / 袁鑫工程顾问（上海）事务所 / 重庆纬图景观设计有限公司 / 株式会社ユニオン / 株式会社 資生堂 / 大成建設株式会社
素材協力：株式会社門脇木材 / 株式会社 山大 / 大光電機株式会社 / 株式会社サンゲツ / 株式会社小林石材工業

❙ 藤原徹平「ストリート ガーデン シアター」
会場：旧こどもの城前（東京都渋谷区神宮前5-53-1）
協賛：株式会社エヌ・シー・エヌ / 株式会社FORM GIVING
植栽協力：産業労働局
設計：フジワラテッペイアーキテクツラボ 藤原徹平、中村駿太、Patrick Wheare、稲田玲奈、寺内玲、久米雄志
構造設計：NATURAL SENSE 池田昌弘＋株式会社エヌ・シー・エヌ 福田浩史、伊藤真治、岡本悠佑、菊池裕香
施工：株式会社エムテック 小澤睦 / スーパーロボット 細川鉄也、加藤良一
リサーチ・プログラム企画：山川陸＋板倉勇人＋伊澤沙里＋フジワラテッペイアーキテクツラボ
ジン・グラフィック制作：美山有＋フジワラテッペイアーキテクツラボ

❙ 会田誠「東京城」
会場：明治神宮外苑 いちょう並木入口（東京都港区北青山2丁目1番地先）
協力：ミヅマアートギャラリー / 秦永ダンボール
施工アドバイザー：株式会社加藤架設 / 株式会社エムテック
設計サポート：フジワラテッペイアーキテクツラボ　藤原徹平 / GANEMAR　小金丸信光 / 小西泰孝建築構造設計 小西泰孝、丸本健悟

❙ 草間彌生「オブリタレーションルーム」
会場：渋谷区役所 第二美竹分庁舎（東京都渋谷区渋谷1-18-21）
©YAYOI KUSAMA　Yayoi Kusama / The obliteration room 2002–present
Collaboration between Yayoi Kusama and Queensland Art Gallery.
Commissioned Queensland Art Gallery. Gift of the artist through the Queensland Art Gallery Foundation 2012
Collection: Queensland Art Gallery, Australia
協力：オオタファインアーツ
設計サポート：フジワラテッペイアーキテクツラボ 藤原徹平、恩田福子、久米雄志 / 甘糟ユリ
素材協力：大光電機株式会社 / 東リ株式会社 / 株式会社タニタハウジングウエア / 日本ペイント株式会社 / 畳屋 よこうち / 株式会社LIXIL
施工：株式会社TANK

❙ 真鍋大度＋Rhizomatiks "2020–2021"
会場：ワタリウム美術館 向かい側の空地（東京都渋谷区神宮前3-41-5）
コンセプト：真鍋大度
テクニカルディレクション：石橋素
ハードウェア開発：毛利恭平
LED プレイヤー：浅井裕太
画像生成 / テキスト生成：2bit
テクニカルサポート：望月俊孝
プロジェクトマネジメント：小幡倫世
プロデューサー：井上貴生

❙ 関連イベント
「パビリオン・トウキョウ2021展 at ワタリウム美術館」
会期：2021年6月19日（土）–9月5日（日）
参加クリエイター：藤森照信、妹島和世、藤本壮介、平田晃久、石上純也、藤原徹平、会田誠
企画 / 会場：ワタリウム美術館（東京都渋谷区神宮前3-7-6）

❙「パビリオン・トウキョウ2021 シンポジウム」
7月2日（金）　18:00–20:00　隈研吾＋藤原徹平＋清野由美（ジャーナリスト）
7月3日（土）　15:00–17:00　進士五十八＋妹島和世＋藤原徹平
7月3日（土）　18:00–20:00　米倉誠一郎＋石上純也
7月9日（金）　18:00–20:00　藤森照信＋平田晃久
7月10日（土） 15:00–17:00　会田誠＋岡啓輔（建築家）＋和多利浩一
7月10日（土） 18:00–20:00　藤本壮介＋真鍋大度
当日の映像はワタリウム美術館のYouTubeチャンネルにてご覧いただけます。

本書籍は、「パビリオン・トウキョウ2021」で展示した作品の記録を、新規書き下ろしの寄稿を含めて、編集したものです。

企画 / Planning
WATARI-UM
The Watari Museum of Contemporary Art

特別協賛 / Special sponsors
大林組　JINS

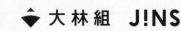

"PAVILION TOKYO 2021" Credits

▌Tokyo Tokyo FESTIVAL Special 13 "PAVILION TOKYO 2021"
Date: July 1st–September 5th, 2021
Venues: Several venues in Tokyo, mainly around National Stadium
Pavilion Creators: Terunobu Fujimori / Kazuyo Sejima / Sou Fujimoto /
Akihisa Hirata / Junya Ishigami / Teppei Fujiwara / Makoto Aida / Yayoi Kusama
Additional Creator: Daito Manabe+Rhizomatiks
Organizers: Tokyo Metropolitan Government, Arts Council Tokyo
(Tokyo Metropolitan Foundation for History and Culture), and Executive
Committee of Pavilion Tokyo 2021
Planning: WATARI-UM, The Watari Museum of Contemporary Art

▌Executive Committee of Pavilion Tokyo 2021
Honorary Chairman: Kengo Kuma (Architect)
Chairperson: Etsuko Watari (Director of WATARI-UM, The Watari Museum of
Contemporary Art)
Members: Ken Hasebe (Mayor of Shibuya Ward) / Kenichi Yoshizumi (Mayor of
Shinjuku Ward) / Masaaki Takei (Mayor of Minato Ward) /
Isoya Shinji (President of Fukui Prefectural University and landscape architect) /
Seiichiro Yonekura (Economist)
Chairman of Production Committee: Koichi Watari (CEO of WATARI-UM,
The Watari Museum of Contemporary Art)
Art Director: groovisions
Event Management: earth garden / en Ltd.
Interviews with creators, production of maps for the guidebook, and publication
of the documentary book: TOTO Publishing
Lawyer: Tasuku Mizuno (CITY LIGHTS LAW)
Auditor: Makoto Sakaki (Mutsuo Yamagishi Tax Accountant Office)

▌SPONSORS
Special Sponsors: OBAYASHI CORPORATION / JINS HOLDINGS Inc.
Sponsors: TOHO LEO Corporation / New Constructor's Network Co.,LTD /
Cartier / Avex Business Development Inc. / FORM GIVING INC. / Nakagawa
Chemical Inc. / Beijing Yihuida Architectural Concrete Engineering Co.,Ltd. /
XinY structural consultants / ChongQing Weitu Landscape Design Co.,Ltd. /
JVCKENWOOD Victor Entertainment Corporation / UNION CORPORATION
JAPAN / SHISEIDO CO., LTD. / TAISEI CORPORATION
Cart support / Providing water: Kakuichi Co., Ltd
Security support: Goto Security Services Company Ltd

▌Terunobu Fujimori: Tea House "Go-an"
Venue: In front of Victor Studio, 2-21-1, Jingumae, Shibuya-ku, Tokyo
Tea house construction: Hideki Kawamoto (Kawamoto Furniture Production
Laboratory)
Base design: Nobumichi Ohshima (Ohshima Atelier)
Base construction: Takahide Miyashima (Miyashima Corporation CO.,LTD.)
Greenery construction: Takehiko Ohbayashi (Ohbayashi Environmental
Technology Institute CO.,LTD.)
Cooperation for tea house construction: Kogakuin University Shiro Ouchida Studio

▌Kazuyo Sejima: Suimei
Venue: Hama-rikyu Gardens (Site of Enryo-kan), Hama rikyu-teien, Chuo-ku, Tokyo
Construction cooperation: KUDO construction company / OOTWO Co.,Ltd /
click Co.,Ltd
Material cooperation: LINTEC SIGN SYSTEM, INC.

▌Sou Fujimoto: Cloud pavilion
Venue 1: Yoyogi Park (near Panorama Grass Field), Yoyogi-Kamizonocho, Jinnan
2chome, Shibuya-ku, Tokyo
Venue 2: Takanawa Gateway Station (inside the ticket gate), 2-1-220, Konan,
Minato-ku, Tokyo
Venue cooperation: East Japan Railway Company
Construction cooperation: Tanaka Koumuten Co., Ltd.
Balloon making: Clown bee
Structural design: Mitsuhiro Kanada (professor, Department of Architecture, Tokyo
University of The Arts)+TECTONICA INC.

▌Akihisa Hirata: Global Bowl
Venue: In front of United Nations University, 5-53-70, Jingumae, Shibuya-ku, Tokyo
Structural design: Mitsuhiro Kanada (professor, Department of Architecture,
Tokyo University of The Arts)
Construction cooperation: Shelter Co., Ltd.
Lighting cooperation: DAIKO ELECTRIC CO.,LTD.

▌Junya Ishigami: Kokage-gumo
Venue: Garden of kudan house, 1-15-9, Kudankita, Chiyoda-ku, Tokyo
Sponsors: TOHO LEO Corporation / Cartier / Nakagawa Chemical Inc. / Beijing
Yihuida Architectural Concrete Engineering Co.,Ltd. / XinY structural consultants /
ChongQing Weitu Landscape Design Co.,Ltd. / UNION CORPORATION JAPAN /
SHISEIDO CO., LTD. / TAISEI CORPORATION
Material support: Kadowaki Co., Ltd / Yamadai Corporation / DAIKO ELECTRIC
CO.,LTD. / Sangetsu Corporation / KOBAYASHI SEKIZAI

▌Teppei Fujiwara: STREET GARDEN THEATER
Venue: In front of the former "National Children's Castle", 5-53-1, Jingumae,
Shibuya-ku, Tokyo
Sponsors: New Constructor's Network Co., LTD / FORM GIVING CORPORATION
Planting cooperation: Bureau of Industrial and Labor Affairs
Design: FUJIWALABO Teppei Fujiwara, Shunta Nakamura, Patrick Wheare,
Rena Inada, Rei Terauchi, Yushi Kume
Structural design: NATURAL SENSE Masahiro Ikeda+New Constructor's
Network Co., LTD Hiroshi Fukuta, Shinji Ito, Yusuke Okamoto, Yuuka Kikuchi
Construction: MTEQ. LTD Mutsumi Ozawa / super robot Tetsuya Hosokawa,
Ryoichi Kato
Research program planning: Rick Yamakawa+Hayato Itakura+Sally Izawa+
FUJIWALABO
ZINE and Graphic design: Yu Miyama+FUJIWALABO

▌Makoto Aida: Tokyo Castle
Venue: Ginkgo Avenue in Meiji Jingu Gaien, 2-1 Kita Aoyama, Minato-ku, Tokyo
Cooperation: MIZUMA ART GALLERY / Sinei Cardboard Co., Ltd.
Construction advisers: Kato Kasetsu Corporation / MTEQ. LTD
Design supporters: FUJIWALABO Teppei Fujiwara / GANEMAR Nobumitsu
Koganemaru / Konishi Structural Engineers. Yasutaka Konishi, Kengo Marumoto

▌Yayoi Kusama: The Obliteration Room
Venue: Shibuya City Office No.2 Mitake Office, 1-18-21 Shibuya, Shibuya-ku, Tokyo
©YAYOI KUSAMA Yayoi Kusama / The obliteration room 2002–present
Collaboration between Yayoi Kusama and Queensland Art Gallery.
Commissioned Queensland Art Gallery. Gift of the artist through the Queensland
Art Gallery Foundation 2012
Collection: Queensland Art Gallery, Australia
Cooperation: OTA FINE ARTS
Design supporters: FUJIWALABO Teppei Fujiwara, Fukuko Onda,
Yushi Kume / Yuri Amakasu
Material cooperation: DAIKO ELECTRIC CO.,LTD. / TOLI Corporation /
TANITA HOUSINGWARE CO., LTD / Nippon Paint Co., Ltd. /
Tatamiya Yokouchi / LIXIL Corporation
Construction: TANK

▌Daito Manabe+Rhizomatiks: "2020-2021"
Venue: Open space in front of WATARI-UM, 3-41-5, Jingumae, Shibuya-ku, Tokyo
Concept: Daito Manabe
Technical Direction: Motoi Ishibashi
Hardware Development: Kyohei Mouri
LED player: Yuta Asai
Image generation, Text generation: 2bit
Technical support: Toshitaka Mochizuki
Project Management: Tomoyo Obata
Producer: Takao Inoue

▌Related event
"PAVILION TOKYO 2021 exhibition at WATARI-UM"
Date: June 19–September 5, 2021
Participating Creators: Terunobu Fujimori / Kazuyo Sejima / Sou Fujimoto /
Akihisa Hirata / Junya Ishigami / Teppei Fujiwara / Makoto Aida
Venue: WATARI-UM, The Watari Museum of Contemporary Art, 3-7-6, Jingumae,
Shibuya-ku, Tokyo

▌"Symposium for PAVILION TOKYO 2021"
July 2nd (Fri) 18:00–20:00 Kengo Kuma+Teppei Fujiwara+Yumi Kiyono (Journalist)
July 3rd (Sat) 15:00–17:00 Isoya Shinji+Kazuyo Sejima+Teppei Fujiwara
July 3rd (Sat) 18:00–20:00 Seichiro Yonekura+Junya Ishigami
July 9th (Fri) 18:00–20:00 Terunobu Fujimori+Akihisa Hirata
July 10th (Sat) 15:00–17:00 Makoto Aida+Keisuke Oka (Architect)+Koichi Watari
July 10th (Sat) 18:00–20:00 Sou Fujimoto+Daito Manabe

The videos can be watched on the WATARI-UM YouTube channel.

本書クレジット

▌写真
後藤秀二：p. 5, pp. 60-61, pp. 96-97, p. 106, p. 119, p. 138左下, p. 139右上, p. 168, p. 170下, p. 171上, p. 172上, pp. 173-175
ToLoLo studio：p. 12, pp. 22-32, pp. 36-37, pp. 44-45, p. 48-52, pp. 62-72, pp. 82-92, p. 95, pp. 100-105, pp. 108-112, pp. 120-121, pp. 124-130, p. 142, p. 144, pp. 146-148, pp. 150-159, p. 162, p. 165, p. 170上, p. 171下, p. 172下
播本和宜：p. 21左上
木奥恵三：p. 21右上・下段4点, p. 81, p. 138中段, p. 139右下, p. 140中段・下段4点, p. 141右上, p. 143, p. 145上, pp. 166-167, p. 188
福林一樹：p. 21 2段目
妹島和世建築設計事務所：pp. 38-39, pp. 42-43
junya.ishigami+associates：p. 107
林琢真デザイン事務所：pp. 122-123
ミヅマアートギャラリー：p. 138上2点・右下

▌マップ、アイコン（"2020-2021" 以外）：groovisions

▌図版掲載協力
東日本旅客鉄道株式会社：p. 57

▌英訳
谷理佐：p. 94
パビリオン・トウキョウ2021 実行委員会：p. 195, p. 197
坂本和子：上記以外

▌英文校正
織部晴崇 坂本和子による英訳部分

▌和文校正
株式会社 鷗来堂

▌初出
GA DOCUMENT 158（エーディーエー・エディタ・トーキョー、2021年）：p. 94

Credits

▌Photographs
Shuji Goto: p. 5, pp. 60-61, pp. 96-97, p. 106, p. 119, p. 138 bottom left, p. 139 top right, p. 168, p. 170 bottom, p. 171 top, p. 172 top, pp. 173-175
ToLoLo studio: p. 12, pp. 22-32, pp. 36-37, pp. 44-45, p. 48-52, pp. 62-72, pp. 82-92, p. 95, pp. 100-105, pp. 108-112, pp. 120-121, pp. 124-130, p. 142, p. 144, pp. 146-148, pp. 150-159, p. 162, p. 165, p. 170 top, p. 171 bottom, p. 172 bottom
Kazunori Hatamoto: p. 21 top left
Keizo Kioku: p. 21 top right / third row / bottom row 4 photos, p. 81, p. 138 middle row, p. 139 bottom right, p. 140 middle row / bottom row 4 photos, p. 141 top right, p. 143, p. 145 top, pp. 166-167, p. 188
Kazuki Fukubayashi: p. 21 second row
Kazuyo Sejima & Associates: pp. 38-39, pp. 42-43
junya.ishigami + associates: p. 107
Takuma Hayashidesign office: pp. 122-123
Mizuma Art Gallery: p. 138 top row 2 photos / bottom right

▌Map/Icon design (excluding "2020-2021"): groovisions

▌Cooperation
East Japan Railway Company: p. 57

▌English translation
Lisa Tani: p. 94
Executive Committee of Pavilion Tokyo 2021: p. 195, p. 197
Kazuko Sakamoto: All pages other than the above.

▌English proofreading
Harutaka Oribe: All English texts translated by Kazuko Sakamoto.

▌Japanese proofreading
OURAIDOU K. K.

▌Original publication
GA DOCUMENT 158, A.D.A. EDITA Tokyo, 2021: p. 94

パビリオン・トウキョウ 2021

2022年3月15日　初版第1刷発行

監修：和多利恵津子（ワタリウム美術館）
編集：TOTO出版
発行者：伊藤剛士
発行所：TOTO出版（TOTO株式会社）
〒107-0062 東京都港区南青山1-24-3 TOTO乃木坂ビル2F
[営業] TEL: 03-3402-7138　FAX: 03-3402-7187
[編集] TEL: 03-3497-1010
URL: https://jp.toto.com/publishing

デザイン：林琢真、蒲原早奈美（林琢真デザイン事務所）
印刷・製本：株式会社サンニチ印刷

ISBN978-4-88706-396-9

PAVILION TOKYO 2021

First published in Japan on March 15, 2022

Editorial Supervision: Etsuko Watari, WATARI-UM, The Watari Museum of Contemporary Art
Editorial: TOTO Publishing
Publisher: Takeshi Ito
TOTO Publishing (TOTO LTD.)
TOTO Nogizaka Bldg., 2F
1-24-3 Minami-Aoyama, Minato-kuTokyo 107-0062, Japan
[Sales] Telephone: +81-3-3402-7138 Facsimile: +81-3-3402-7187
[Editorial] Telephone: +81-3-3497-1010
URL: https://jp.toto.com/publishing
Designer: Takuma Hayashi Sanami Kamohara (Hayashi Takuma Design Office.)
Printer: Sannichi Printing Co., Ltd

ISBN978-4-88706-396-9